W -4 5

Jim Harris
1973

The Witness of the Spirit

Other books by the same author:—

THE CHRISTIAN VIEW OF SCIENCE AND SCRIPTURE

TYPES OF APOLOGETIC SYSTEMS

PROTESTANT BIBLICAL INTERPRETATION

PROTESTANT CHRISTIAN EVIDENCES

THE PATTERN OF RELIGIOUS AUTHORITY

THE WITNESS
OF THE SPIRIT

*An Essay on the Contemporary
Relevance of the Internal
Witness of the Holy Spirit*

by

BERNARD RAMM, B.D., M.A., Ph. D.

*Wm. B. Eerdmans Publishing Company
Grand Rapids, Michigan*

Except for an occasional free translation, all quotations of Scripture are from the Revised Standard Version of the Bible, copyrighted 1946 and 1952 by the Division of Christian Education of the National Council of Churches, and used by permission.

DEDICATION

To Elizabeth and Stephen, who have taught me more than I have taught them

PREFACE

The impulse to write this book comes directly from writing *The Pattern of Religious Authority*. In working through the materials for that book it became apparent that the doctrine of the internal witness of the Holy Spirit had almost disappeared from evangelical literature and theology, and that this disappearance was unfortunate for both the spirit and methodology of that theology. The second impulse came from the opportunity to read French and German materials while at the University of Basel (1957-1958).

I have refrained from excessive documentation and quotation. Such a procedure has its place in some types of scholarly work but it does not serve a purpose in every kind of production. My intention has been to present the heart of the matter. Those who wish for greater detail may consult the works listed in the bibliography. For the sake of greater clarity and forcefulness in the argument I felt that a measure of repetition was necessary. I trust that the reader will concur in this judgment.

It was Pascal who said that every author was indebted to other authors and ought to speak of "our book," not "my book." And this book is gratefully "our book," not "my book." Although it is not always apparent, my constant companions have been my Greek New Testament; Arndt and Gingrich's *Greek-English Lexicon of the New Testament;* and Dr. Alfred Schmoller's *Handkonkordanz zum griechischen Neuen Testament.*

Whenever I have cited Calvin's *Institutes,* I have simply put the Book, Chapter, and Paragraph in parentheses. I have also employed the Greek word *plērophoria* without always translating it. It means fullness of conviction, and I have used this word to specify that state of conviction about the truth which is produced in the mind of the believer by the Holy Spirit. The word *testimonium* stands everywhere for the fuller expression, "the internal witness of the Holy Spirit."

7

CONTENTS

"My own complaint against most writers on the Holy Spirit is that they know too much." *A correspondent*

"The need of divine guidance is never more deeply felt than when one undertakes to give instruction in the work of the Holy Spirit — so unspeakably tender is the subject, touching the inmost secrets of God and the soul's deepest mysteries." *Kuyper*

"Among all the points of doctrine which distinguish the Reformed Churches from the Church of Rome on the one hand, and from the Sects on the other hand, the doctrine of the inner witness of the Holy Spirit is perhaps one of the most delicate to grasp and one of the most difficult to discuss." *Preiss*

"The Reformers, setting opposite to the bondage of the will and the sin of man the all-powerful grace of God, never said at any time that man was justified by freedom nor by authority nor by reason nor by anything exterior or human, but by the action of the Holy Spirit, by the acceptance of the sacrifice of Jesus Christ, by the communion of the heart with God." *Pannier*

"The dispensation of the Spirit — *hē diakonia tou pneumatos.*" *Paul, II Cor. 3:8*

CHAPTER I

HISTORICAL ROOTS

Section 1: *The paper pope?*[1]

Few assertions are more superficial than this, that the Reformers substituted a paper pope for the living pope. From the servitude of an authoritative person, it is alleged, they moved to the servitude of a book; fleeing one yoke, they managed only to take upon themselves another, the lordship of an historically conditioned book.

Such a criticism is wide of the mark. The center of the great debate between Catholics and Reformers did not concern the authority of the Scriptures as such, which they both accepted. To be sure, there was disagreement on certain points: the extent of the canon — the Catholics maintaining the canonicity of the Apocrypha; the principles of hermeneutics — the Catholics maintaining the validity of the fourfold method of the scholastics; and the relationship of Church to Scripture — the Catholics making the Church the custodian and therefore the lord of the Scriptures. But certainly each party, in its own way, recognized the authority of "the book."

The real life-and-death struggle was at two points: the relation of Scripture to the Church, and the source of the Christian's certainty that the Scriptures are the Word of God. With reference to the first point, Calvin placed the Scriptures above the Church, whereas Romanism placed them under the Church. Calvin insisted that the Church is governed by the Word and the Spirit, and

---

1 For Calvin's own position see *Institutes*, I, vii, viii, and ix; and *Letter to Sadolet*. The most thorough work on Calvin's doctrine of the witness of the Spirit is: W. Krusche, *Das Wirken des Heiligen Geistes nach Calvin*. Other relevant works are: B. Warfield, *Calvin and Augustine;* W. Neisel, *The Theology of John Calvin;* G. Hendry, *The Holy Spirit in Christian Theology;* R. E. Davies, *The Problem of Authority in the Continental Reformers.*

therefore must be in subjection to the Scriptures. All traditions and the entire ecclesiastical hierarchy must submit to this lordship. With reference to the second point, Calvin replaced the voice of the Church, which supposedly tells us with great assurance that the Scriptures are the Word of God, with the *internal witness of the Holy Spirit*.[2] The Bible itself teaches, said Calvin, that when God gives his revelation, he gives along with it a certainty that it *is* revelation. When speaking of the revelation given the Patriarchs, Calvin asserts that God so inwardly persuaded and impressed them that they were convinced that the doctrine received by them was from God (*Institutes*, I, vi, 2). The particular structure of this inward persuading, of this firm conviction, is the inward witness of the Holy Spirit, the *testimonium spiritus sancti*.

Where Calvin derived this doctrine is not known. It appears only in seed form in the first edition of the *Institutes*, so we may infer that he did not enter into his Protestant faith with this doctrine fully developed. R. E. Davies suggests that Calvin's theory of the *testimonium* was a deduction from his conversion experience.[3] J. Pannier says that Calvin did not derive it from a study of the Fathers or scholastics, but from his diligent study of the Scriptures.[4]

In developing his doctrine of the *testimonium* Calvin was faced with three alternative theories. Christian certainty was explained by Romanism as the gift of an infallible Church to the believing Catholic. The enthusiasts, or fanatics, found their certainty of faith in an immediate revelation of the Holy Spirit, a revelation which was not bound to the contents of Scripture. And some apologists were asserting that they could demonstrate the truthfulness of the Christian faith by purely rational evidences. Calvin was unhappy with all three theories, and developed his doctrine of the *testimonium* in opposition to each of them.

---

2 Throughout the remainder of this book the word *testimonium* stands for this entire phrase.

3 *Op. cit.*, p. 100.

4 J. Pannier, *Le Témoignage du Saint-Esprit*, pp. 70-72.

He opposed rationalistic Christian apologetics for several reasons.[5] To begin with, the Scriptures themselves do not agree with this method, for the prophets and apostles do not appeal to rational arguments, but to the sacred name of God (I,vii,4). A rational apologetics gives human assurance where only divine assurance is suitable (I,vii,4). Such proofs are matters of probable supposition, the product of disputation, and the human mind is always left in suspense with such proofs. Calvin says that even if he debated with a man and convinced him of the truthfulness of the faith, the man would not have any substantial assurance (I,viii,1).

Furthermore, the darkness of the human mind prevents it from being a fit instrument to prove the divinity of the Christian faith. In fact, such an attempt is preposterous (I,vii,4). The philosophers' attempt to "penetrate the heavens" only arouses Calvin's scorn, for upon inspection of their findings he discovers them to be "fading colors" (I,v,12). And, writing to Sadolet, he says that the Christian faith is not to be propped up by human testimony or doubtful opinion; it is not to be based on human authority, but it is something engraved on the heart by the finger of the living God, and thus is so certain that it cannot be obliterated by deceitful error.[6] Calvin's conclusion at the end of his own positive discussion of Christian evidences is that "such alone are not sufficient to produce firm faith," and are "only secondary aids to our imbecility." Those Christians who wish to convert the infidels by Christian evidences alone "betray great folly" (I,viii,13).

According to Romanism it was an infallible society, the Church, which declared the Scriptures to be the Word of God. Thus the Catholic believer, confused by the conflicting voices in religion and uncertain about the Bible because of its mysterious character, could find certainty in the voice of the Church.

5 Cf. *Institutes*, I, viii, "Rational Proofs to Establish the Belief of the Scripture." This is one of the most debated subjects today in Calvin study.

6 *Reply to Sadolet*.

Calvin's opposition to Romanism can be summarized in four objections:

(i) The voice of the Church concerning the divinity of Scripture is nonetheless the voice of man, and therefore rests precariously upon human authority (I,vii,1 and I, vii, 3). In attempting to speak for the Bible, the Church shows great contempt for the Holy Spirit. Furthermore, the voice of the Church comes from outside of man, and thus is not superior to the read word or the preached sermon. Only an inner voice can give the needed assurance.

(ii) To say that the Church must guarantee the authority of the Scriptures is to deny the *majesty* (this is Calvin's favorite word for the inspired quality of the Bible), and the *autopistia* of the Scriptures. Scripture is Scripture in itself, just as black is black in itself and sugar is sweet in itself. Sugar cannot be made sweet by Church fiat, nor can the Church add black to black. The Scriptures, begotten by the Holy Spirit, are thus Scriptures in themselves, i.e., they are autopistic. The test of their divinity is within themselves; it is not in the Church. The Church cannot declare something to be Scripture which is not Scripture; and if something is Scripture, it is Scripture in itself and does not need the dictum of the Church to make it so.

(iii) The Church was a group of redeemed men before it was an hierarchy or an institution. These men were redeemed through the Word of God. Therefore the foundation of the Church is in the prophets and the apostles. Without the Word of God there would be no foundation, and hence no Church. Therefore the Word of God has priority over the Church. It is wrong for the Church to be lord of Scripture when Scripture is the foundation of the Church. It is the Word of God which tells us that we are the Church, and not the Church which tells us that the Scriptures are the Word of God.

(iv) The sign of the Church, according to Sadolet, is the presence of the Spirit. Calvin counters by saying that the sign of the Church is the Word of God. The Romanists' position is a separating of Word from Spirit, and this is a great sacrilege. It is true that God governs the Church by his Spirit; but to prevent this government from being vaguely defined, the Spirit governs *by* the Word. Therefore the sign of the Church is not a mere claim to have the Spirit, but a concrete manifestation of government by the Word of God. The Roman Catholic Church affronts the Holy Spirit when it does not govern itself by the Word. Rather, Romanism buries the Word of God by her traditions and replaces the Word with falsehoods.[7]

The third possible source of verifying the Christian faith would be by a direct experience of revelation — a revelation so real and concrete that it would not need the Bible. This claim of the enthusiasts was treated by Calvin in *Institutes* I, ix: "The Fanaticism Which Disregards the Scripture." Calvin has three things to say to these enthusiasts:

(i) This is the same error of Romanism in a different setting: it is an illicit separation of Word from Spirit. Calvin says to them: "For the Lord hath established a kind of mutual connection between the certainty of his word and of his Spirit; so that our minds are filled with a solid reverence for the word, when by the light of the Spirit we are enabled therein to behold the Divine countenance" (I,ix,3). The revelations of the enthusiasts then represent a separation of Word from Spirit, *a union which God has established.* To separate them is "detestable sacrilege" (I,ix,3). There is no revelation apart from the Scriptures, for the Lord gives his children illumination by the Spirit *through the Word* (I,ix,3).

(ii) The ways and doings of the Holy Spirit are set forth in an image in Scripture. All actions of the Holy Spirit conform to this image, for the Spirit is consistent with himself. But the enthusiasts, in claiming revelations apart from the Word of God, give us an image of the Spirit not found in the Scriptures. This spirit is not the Spirit of God, but a devilish spirit.

(iii) The revelations of the enthusiasts have material *content.* They are revelation in the primary sense of that word, namely, the communication of knowledge. But this is contrary to the entire structure of the *testimonium.*

7 *Ibid.*

"The office of the Spirit, then, which is promised to us, is not to feign new and unheard-of revelations, or to coin a new system of doctrine, which would seduce us from the received doctrine of the Gospel, but to seal to our minds the same doctrine which the Gospel delivers" (I,ix,1). Thus the *testimonium* is no revelation as such, but works in connection with an already existing revelation. To really receive the benefits of the Spirit — which the enthusiasts want so much — they must diligently "read and attend to Scripture" (I,ix,2).

The conclusion, then, is that in the Christian religion our certainty is not derived from the rational powers of the human mind, nor from the word of the imperial church, nor from the direct delivery of a revelation within the heart. Rather, it comes only from the *testimonium spiritus sancti*.

In developing his positive doctrine of the *testimonium*, Calvin begins with four presuppositions which we may note at the outset:

(i) The incomprehensibility of God on the one side ("his essence is indeed incomprehensible" — I,v,1), and man's finitude on the other, call for a special action of God in breaking through to us. This breaking through, subjectively considered, is the operation of the Holy Spirit.

(ii) The human mind is corrupted. Sin has made it blind and perverse. It has lost its inward spiritual vision and cannot read the plainest revelation of God. Its original knowledge of God is replaced by every sort of religious fancy. It is a labyrinth, and man wanders around in the labyrinth of his mind without ever finding the truth of God. Only a divine act can bring light into this darkness.

(iii) About divine things there must be a divine certainty. Divine things must be known in such a way that all doubt is removed (I,vii,1). The believer must hear the words of Scripture as if God himself pronounced them (I,vii,1). There is no real faith until we are indubitably persuaded by God himself (I,vii,4); and we cannot say that we really believe Scripture until God has placed its authority beyond all controversy.

(iv) In the course of his thought Calvin developed his doctrine of the union of Word and Spirit. We see it very clearly in his famous *Reply to Sadolet* as well as in his refutation of the enthusiasts in *Institutes* I, ix. This union is impressively stated in the short work, *Summary of Doctrine concerning the Ministry of the Word and the Sacraments*,[8] but unfortunately its authenticity cannot be established. However, it reflects Calvin's doctrine from authentic sources.

The union of Word and Spirit is the theological ground for Calvin's theory of the *testimonium*. The Holy Spirit is the *internal* minister of the Word who speaks the compelling and persuasive Word to the human heart.[9] When the word spoken by the *external* minister of the Word penetrates the ear of the listener, the internal minister speaks it to the heart. The Spirit efficaciously impresses the Word upon our hearts, and at that moment the word becomes to us the Word of life (I,ix,3), for it is the function of the Spirit to enlighten and impress the heart with the Word.[10]

Because there is this union, the workings of the Spirit always agree with the image of the Spirit in the Word. This means that the *testimonium* is but one function of the work of the Spirit — an important one, but not the only one. Calvin declares that the benefits of Christ are conveyed to us by the same inner workings of the Spirit (III,i). If we are to partake of the blessings of the Spirit, we must read the Word of God (I,ix,2).

Since these subjects will be treated in detail later, we give here only a brief résumé of Calvin's theory of the *testimonium*.

(i) Prior to the *testimonium* there existed concrete, historical acts of God for human redemption, and their documentation in Sacred Scripture. The acts of God are the ultimate reality, and the Scriptures contain a faithful account of them. The *testimonium* is directed toward these two items, and therefore is a sequel in point of time.

(ii) The *testimonium* is a species of persuasion. It is the *cause* of our persuasion, not the *ground*. The ground is the truth of God, namely, the inspired, autopistic Scrip-

8 *The Library of Christian Classics*, XXII, 171-177.
9 *Ibid.*, p. 174.
10 *Tracts*, II, 250.

ture. At this point Calvin does not face Romanism with the witness of the Spirit but with the inspired Scripture. The Scripture is the Scripture because it is inspired, but we are powerless to see it as such. "Our minds are too rude to be able to grasp the spiritual wisdom of God and our hearts are too prone to distrust, or [too prone] to perverse confidence in ourselves or other creatures to rest of their own accord in God."[11] When profane men read the Scriptures, it is to them so much more religious opinion (I,vii,4). Therefore we need a special persuasion that we may see the Scriptures as the Word of God. Our powerlessness is the powerlessness of man and not a defect of Sacred Scripture.

Because the *testimonium* is a persuasion, it is a persuasion about something. It is not its own content. The *testimonium* is a revealing action, not a revealed content. It is an illumination, not a communication. For this reason Calvin opposed the enthusiasts who claimed a revelation *with a content*.

(iii) It is an *absolute* persuasion. It is an illumination "by an internal revelation of God" (I,v,14); we have an "indubitable persuasion" (I,vii,4); it is a "clear demonstration" (I,vii,4); it is reading the Scriptures with "pure eyes and sound minds" (I,vii,4); the "Spirit . . . penetrates our hearts to convince us" (I,vii,4); it is a sealing, an earnest, an illumination (I,vii,4); it is being "confirmed by the Spirit" (I,vii,5); it is "an intuitive perception of God himself" (I,vii,5); it is a "persuasion" (I,vii,5); it is a "revelation from heaven" (I,vii,5); it is an "alacrity to hear the voice of God" (I,vii,5); it is an "internal persuasion of the Holy Spirit" (I,viii,13); it is a seal to our minds of the doctrine of the gospel (I,ix, 1); it is an efficacious impressing of the heart (I,ix,3); it is the "light of the Spirit" (I,ix,3); and it cannot be effaced (III,ii,12).

(iv) It has been thought by some that Calvin had two witnesses — one to the Word of God and one to our salvation. Others have said that Calvin teaches that we are

11 "Catechism of the Church of Geneva," *Library of Christian Classics*, XXII, 105.

first persuaded that the Scriptures are true, then persuaded to believe its Gospel. W. Krusche shows that this is not the case.[12] This would mean a separation of the Scriptures as a book from the Scriptures as containing a content. But the *testimonium* is given with the content of Scripture, i.e., Jesus Christ and his gospel. In a very important sentence Calvin says that the Scriptures become the Word of life to the believer when impressed on our hearts by the Holy Spirit, *when the Scriptures exhibit Christ* (I,ix,3). To have two witnesses would drastically separate Word and content; and to say that we first believe the Scripture, then the gospel, is a similarly drastic and fateful separation of Word and content.

This is why Calvin makes the preaching of the Word so important. It is actually a means of grace. Why? Because the preaching contains the content of the Scripture, Jesus Christ; and the *testimonium* occurs during preaching. Consequently those scholars who think that Calvin taught two witnesses have no explanation for Calvin's doctrine of preaching as a means of grace. Furthermore, Calvin's teaching that the *testimonium* existed before the Scriptures were written is fatal to the notion that for him the *testimonium* is sheer validation of Scripture apart from its content.

(v) Finally, this *testimonium* is addressed to the total man. Certainly faith is knowledge, according to Calvin, because it is faith in a revelation, in a gospel, in a truth of God. But it is also a trust. Calvin wrote very strongly against faith as intellectualism (III,viii). Faith brings *all* of us unto *all* of God's redemption. Therefore the *testimonium* confronts and works upon the total man.

Section 2: *Martin Luther*

Luther's concern with the doctrine of the Holy Spirit, and particularly the witness of the Spirit, grows out of different historical and personal connections than that of Calvin. Further, it is Loetscher's claim that Luther did not work out a systematic doctrine of the witness of the Spirit, but that his doctrine of faith directly implied

12 *Op. cit.*, pp. 216ff.

it.[13] Luther apparently accepted Augustine's distinction
of the *inner* and *outer* Word of God and in connection
with this it is not difficult to associate the *testimonium*
with the inner Word. Whatever differences Luther and
Calvin may have had in regard to the *testimonium* and
the relation of Word to Spirit, they were one in their
belief in the reality and necessity of the *testimonium*.
In his *Small Catechism* Luther wrote: "I believe that I
cannot by my own reason or strength believe in Jesus
Christ my Lord, or come to him; but the Holy Ghost has
called me through the Gospel, enlightened me by his
gifts, and sanctified and preserved me in true faith."

Luther is especially interested in showing how it is the
Holy Spirit who takes the risen Christ out of the realm
of mere idea and history and makes him a present reality
to the consciousness of the believer. The human person
with his will, reason, and powers, can grasp Christ only
as idea, i.e., as so many statements that he taught certain
things and claimed certain things; or as history, namely,
that this person existed at such a time and place. These
human powers cannot take Christ out of the realm of
idea and history. It is the Holy Spirit who makes Christ
a reality to the believer. The center of the *testimonium*
is Christ. Concerning the intimate relationship of the
Spirit and Christ, Prenter writes: "Luther does not know
any other Spirit than the Spirit of Christ: that Spirit in
which the living Christ is with us. And the living Christ
manifests himself to us only in the Spirit; there is no
other living Christ."[14] Thus the witness of the Spirit
is precisely the taking of Christ out of the domain of
historical faith and making him the reality he is in
justifying faith.

This action of the Spirit in making Christ really present to the believer is always in connection with the Word
of God. Luther, as much as Calvin, believed in the inspiration of Scripture and therefore in its *autopistia*. Luther calls the Word the window and the door of the Spirit

13 W. Loetscher, "Luther and the Problem of Authority," *The
Princeton Theological Review*, XI (1918), p. 508. Paralleling
Krusche's work on Calvin and the Holy Spirit is Regin Prenter's
Spiritus Creator on Luther's doctrine of the Holy Spirit.

14 *Op. cit.*, p. 61.

whereby he makes his entry into the heart of the believer. Thus in the union of Word and Spirit, Luther and Calvin are also one although their followers developed different emphases.

The actual bringing of Christ to the consciousness of the believer by the Spirit through the Word results in an "experience." By "experience" Luther did not mean "religious experience," but rather that act whereby the Holy Spirit takes Christ out of the realm of idea and history and makes him a reality to the believer. This is no metaphysical something, but is the direct action of God himself, the working of the Holy Spirit of God.

According to Luther the Word without the Spirit is mere letter, mere law, mere writing. It is in itself, to be sure, the Word of God, but to the heart untouched by the Spirit it is like any other book. However, there is this exception: it is the Word of God with power, even if everybody is asleep while it is preached![15] The Lord must speak his inner Word to the inner ear if the Word of God is to be heard as the Word of God. Concerning this point Prenter writes: "Hereby we really state this one thing: the Word of God — or the gospel — is not just present in Scripture in such a way that it can be unmistakably pointed out. If God does not speak into the heart while the ear listens to the outward Word, the outward Word remains the word of man and law. When we hear the Word of the Scripture, we are compelled to wait on the Spirit of God. It is God who has the Scripture in his hand. If God does not infuse his Spirit, the hearer of the Word is not different from the deaf man. No one can rightly understand the Word of God unless he receives it directly from the Holy Spirit."[16]

Luther also uses the *testimonium* against the papacy, especially with reference to the certainty of our salvation.[17] The certainty and assurance of our salvation rests upon the Holy Spirit's inner witness. The Holy Spirit is sent by the Word, and makes the Word a reality to the Christian. The certainty of the divinity of the Word,

15 Cf. Krusche, *op. cit.*, p. 225.
16 *Op. cit.*, p. 102.
17 Cf. his *Commentary on St. Paul's Epistle to the Galatians*, on 4:6.

and the certainty of the salvation it offers, is a certainty given by the Holy Spirit. This stands in sharpest contradistinction to the Roman claim that only by the Church's pronouncement can we have religious certainty. Luther wrote: "Let us therefore give thanks unto God, that we are delivered from this monstrous doctrine or doubting [as fostered by Romanism], and can now assure ourselves that the Holy Ghost crieth and bringeth forth in our hearts unspeakable groanings. . . . Here on the one side [Romanism], doubting and desperation must needs follow: but on the other side [*testimonium*], assurance and joy of the Spirit."[18]

Section 3: Historical considerations

There remains to be written a work on the history of the doctrine of the Holy Spirit that is comprehensive; and a work on the history of the *testimonium* from Luther and Calvin to the present is certainly something to be desired.[19] The Christian Church has always possessed the *testimonium* on the experiential side, even if it did not develop it as a theological doctrine. We are indebted to H. B. Swete's *The Holy Spirit in the Ancient Church* for gathering together the various opinions of the Fathers on the Holy Spirit showing a richness of thought that is not always appreciated.

Athanasius represents a critical turning point. Eventually some Christian theologian would see that the problem of Christ was also the problem of the Holy Spirit,

18 *Loc. cit.*
19 Warfield has a discussion entitled "Historical Relations" in *Calvin and Augustine,* pp. 116ff., and he cites the relevant materials most of which are unimportant. J. Pannier, *Le Témoignage du Saint-Esprit* contains a general history of the doctrine; traces it in its development in Calvin; then among the Jesuits; and then among the French Reformed. From the Lutheran side we have Prof. Klaiber's "Die Lehre der altprotestantischen Dogmatiker von dem *testimonium spiritus sancti* und ihrer dogmatischen Bedeutung," *Jahrbücher für Deutsche Theologie,* II/1, pp. 1-54, 1857. The opinions of the great Lutheran dogmaticians are contained in Schmid, *The Doctrinal Theology of the Evangelical Lutheran Church;* and of the Reformed in Heppe's *Reformed Dogmatics.* Krusche's bibliography has many important titles. *Op. cit.,* pp. 344-348.

and that therefore the Church could not speak a *homoousian* about the Son but withhold it from the Holy Spirit. It was Athanasius who saw this clearly (and of course the Arians in denial!) and drew the proper conclusions, which are preserved for us in his *Letters concerning the Holy Spirit*. The Arian objections to the divinity of the Son applied to the Spirit, and the Arians were not shy in making them known. Athanasius states their belief as follows: "Having denied the Word of God, they naturally say the same evil things against the Spirit." He then replies: "For if they thought correctly of the Word, they would think soundly of the Spirit also, who proceeds from the Father, and, belonging to the Son, is from him given to the disciples and all who believe in him."[20]

Two things may be said of Augustine and the *testimonium*. (i) Although he did not develop the doctrine of the *testimonium* in so many words, his doctrines of the knowledge of God and of divine illumination add up to the *testimonium*. In his doctrine of the saving knowledge of God there is a special act of illumination within the believing mind resulting in a God-given vision of the divine truth. This is essentially the *testimonium*[21] of which Calvin in his own time gave an exegetical and theological treatment. (ii) With his elaborate work on the Trinity, Augustine established the full dignity of the Holy Spirit in the doctrine of God, and the divinity of his actions in salvation. Although Athanasius had already used the Greek word *trias*, and Tertullian the Latin *trinitas*, it was Augustine who formulated the doctrine definitively for all who receive the Christian revelation with believing seriousness.

Before leaving the patristic period it might be well to sample a few of the opinions of the Fathers to show their instinctive sense of the importance of the work of the Holy Spirit. Tertullian speaks of "his Vicar, the Holy Spirit." Irenaeus says, "The Spirit is . . . the ladder by which we ascend to God." Justin Martyr asks, "Will the human intellect ever see God unless it is furnished with the Holy Spirit?" Augustine declares that the Holy

20 *Letters*, I, 20. Shapland translation.
21 Pannier, *op. cit.*, pp. 67ff.

Spirit "is God's gift and who brings us to God." Hippolytus says, "He who gives understanding is the Holy Spirit." Others could be added.[22]

According to Pannier and Warfield there is nothing on the subject before Calvin. J. Baillie, however, has affirmed that when Thomas Aquinas speaks of faith as one of the seven virtues, he comes close to the doctrine of the *testimonium*.[23]

Calvin's doctrine of the *testimonium* was worked out completely in the 1539 edition of the *Institutes* and immediately became the common heritage of Lutheran and Reformed dogmaticians.[24] However, none of the Reformers started with the *testimonium*. It was incipient in their original doctrines and emerged at the proper occasion. It was put in the important creeds (Gallican, Belgian, Second Helvetic, Waldensian, and by implication in The Formula of Concord) and received its finest expression in the Westminster Confession (according to Warfield). It was also appropriated by the Reformed and Lutheran theologians and included in their works. Speaking for the Reformed, Heppe says: "The most essential 'evidence' of the 'certainty of the Scripture' is the testimony of the Holy Spirit. This testimony is unique, proper only to those reborn by the Spirit of Christ and known only to them. And it has such powers that it not only attests and seals abundantly in our souls the truth of the prophetic and apostolic doctrine, but also effectually bends and moves our hearts to embrace and follow it."[25] And speaking for the Lutherans Quenstedt writes: "The ultimate reason by and through which we are led to believe with a divine and unshaken faith that God's Word is God's Word, is the intrinsic power and efficacy of that Word itself, and the testimony and seal of the Holy Spirit, speaking in and through Scripture. Because the bestowment of faith, not only that by which we believe in the articles, but even that by which we believe in the Scriptures, that

22 Selected at random from Swete, *op. cit.*
23 *Our Knowledge of God*, pp. 113-114. Similarly, A. Richardson, *Christian Apologetics*, pp. 213-214.
24 Cf. Warfield, *op. cit.*, pp. 122ff.
25 Heppe, *op. cit.*, p. 24, citing Ursinus.

exhibit and propose the articles, is a work that emanates from the Holy Spirit, or the Supreme Cause."[26]

It is true that certain divisions arose between the Lutheran and the Reformed theologians. The Lutherans gave the *testimonium* an experiential coloring which bothered the Reformed. The Reformed regarded the Scripture as an instrument of the Spirit, inoperative until the Spirit uses it; whereas the Lutherans had more of a sacramental view of Scripture.[27] The Reformed associated the Spirit with the Word very intimately, whereas the Lutheran view appeared to cement the two together.[28] But these are differences in detail and application and do not affect the essence of the *testimonium*.

Arminius included the *testimonium* in his theology (*The Writings of Arminius,* I,40), and judging from Whittaker's *Disputation on Scripture* (1610), the *testimonium* had a good reception among the Anglican divines. The Baptists gave proper regard to the *testimonium* in their earlier confessions. The Second London Confession (Article V) is very similar in wording to The Westminster Confession. The confessions of the Swedes (Article VI), of the French (Article VI), of the Germans (Article VII); the Somerset Confession (Article XIX), the Confession of Faith of 1644 (Article XXII), A Declaration of Faith of English People (Article X), and A Short Confession of Faith (Article XVIII) all either specifically repeat the *testimonium* or speak with such language as to imply it.

The reaction of the Jesuits to the doctrine is one of the curiosities of theological history. There is the famous instance when a Jesuit put the Scriptures to his ear and claimed that he couldn't hear the Holy Spirit speaking — as a child puts a sea shell to its ear to hear the ocean roar! Others of them denied its validity outright, though Pannier gives a list of Jesuits who sought to use the

---

26 Schmid, *op. cit.,* p. 55. See also R. Preus, *The Inspiration of the Scripture,* pp. 108ff.

27 Krusche, *op. cit.,* pp. 218ff.

28 Preus discusses this under "The Union of the Word and the Spirit." *Op. cit.,* pp. 183-190.

doctrine in Catholicism as a secondary and supporting confirmation of Scripture.[29]

The subsequent history of the *testimonium* is a mixed one. Among the orthodox it suffered from four things: (i) it became identified with religious experience and so lost its real force as a persuasion; or (ii) in the development of a rationalistic apologetic there was no genuine place left for the *testimonium;* or (iii) a sense of balance was lost and the *testimonium* was interpreted as a formal validation of Scripture, or the validation of theological propositions without proper regard to Christ or salvation; or (iv) there was a failure to see its critical role in theological methodology.

In religious liberalism from Schleiermacher on, it became equivalent to the autonomy of religious experience. It was no longer a *testimonium* or a persuasion about Scripture and the gospel but a brief for the self-authenticating character of religious experience. Pannier's fine study is frequently marred by the intrusion of the religious liberalism of the French liberal school (under whose auspices the book was written in fulfillment of a doctor's degree).

The *testimonium* has received its best interpretation by the nineteenth-and twentieth-century Reformed theologians in France, Germany, England, and America. Even so, among these men there are great divergences in treatment. With some writers it is not discussed with the principle of authority (although the Westminster Confession is very strong at this point), nor with the inspiration of Scriptures (where a catechetical method prevails). Others confine their remarks to illumination under the general topic of regeneration. With still others it is given passing reference as a great doctrine but is nowhere discussed in their dogmatics. Certainly it was at the heart of Calvin's methodology, for it is developed very early in the *Institutes* and is stoutly maintained in the *Commentaries.* And in Kuyper's *Principles of Sacred Theology,* Lecerf's *An Introduction to Reformed Dogmatics,* and Warfield's "Calvin's Doctrine of the Knowl-

29 *Op. cit.,* pp. 161-163.

edge of God," the *testimonium* is given its rightful place in theological methodology.

The doctrine has received fresh attention from neo-orthodox writers, such as Barth and Brunner. Barth discusses it extensively in his section on "The Outpouring of the Holy Spirit" (*Church Dogmatics*, I/2, Part III). However, followers of the Reformed tradition usually hold that the neo-orthodox doctrines of revelation and inspiration are such that their version of the *testimonium* is essentially faulty.[30]

---

30 Cf. John Murray, "The Attestation of Scripture," *The Infallible Word*, pp. 41ff.

CHAPTER II

FUNDAMENTAL CONSIDERATIONS

Section 4: *The* testimonium *and the Trinity*

The revelation of God eventually unfolds the doctrine of the Trinity, and conversely, the Trinity unfolds itself in revelation. But this revealing or unfolding is not an academic or notarial unfolding. The doctrine of the Trinity comes to us enmeshed in the dynamics of redemption and in the successive inbreaking of revelation. It is the underlying presupposition of every page of Sacred Scripture. It comes to the surface in certain passages, such as the great commission (Matt. 28:19, "in the name of the Father and of the Son and of the Holy Spirit") ; in the apostolic benediction (II Cor. 13:14, "the grace of the Lord Jesus Christ and the love of God and the fellowship of the Holy Spirit") ; and in Paul's "one Spirit, one Lord, one God" (Eph. 4:4-6).

Pressures existed early in the history of the Church to forge a theological formulation which would relate the saving and revealing actions of the Father, the Son, and the Spirit. This was not an easy work, for, like the doctrine of the person of Christ, this doctrine had to be defined against many false positions. For example, the binarians equated the Holy Spirit with the spirit of Jesus Christ. But eventually, through the combined effect of the christological and then pneumatological debates and the creative writing of theology by men like Tertullian, Athanasius, and Augustine, the doctrine of the Trinity was brought to formulation. It took its official form in the Athanasian Creed: "That we worship one God in Trinity and Trinity in Unity, neither confounding the persons nor dividing the substance. . . . In this Trinity there is nothing before or after, nothing greater or less; but the whole three persons are coeternal together and coequal, so that in all things . . . both the Unity in Trinity and the Trinity in Unity is to be worshipped."

Once the doctrine of the Trinity was formulated, the Holy Spirit came into his own in Christian theology. He was invested with full deity and personality. Those heresies which robbed the Spirit of his deity and personality (Arianism and binarianism) were repudiated. Once the doctrine of the Trinity was grasped and formulated, it seemed to be the only natural meaning of Sacred Scripture. It was a doctrine produced by Scripture study and theological debate. And out of this debate and this Bible study the doctrine was clarified. And once a doctrine has been clarified in this manner, it has a wonderful way of explaining Scripture when turned back upon the Scripture. We wonder why we did not see it so clearly before! Yet this is the nature of progress in theology. Only by pushes and pulls, by rushes to one flank and a counter-rush to another flank, does the "obvious" in Scripture become "obvious."

In the *testimonium* we have to do with the Trinity. In this doctrine the deity and the personality of the Spirit are secured, and his action together with the Trinity. Therefore we have to do with a Trinity and a divine person. We have to do with one who acts as God because he is God. We have to do with a divine action because it is the act of a divine person. If the *testimonium* is not seen from the perspective of the Trinity, we do not see it as it must be seen. And when we speak of the witness of the Spirit, we must always remind ourselves that it is the Spirit of the Trinity in Unity and the Unity in Trinity.

The Christian Church has had a problem with theological reflection about the Holy Spirit. The Scriptures make it clear that Christian consciousness must be Christ-consciousness, not Spirit-consciousness. The Spirit leads to Christ; he glorifies Christ; and he teaches us Christ. To repeat a theological truism: there is no pneumatology in Scripture isolated from a christology. Yet the revelation itself reflects upon the Holy Spirit, and therefore Christian theology must reflect upon the Holy Spirit. To understand the totality of the revelation of God we must search out that measure of attention which the revelation gives to the Holy Spirit. Failure to do this results in theological blind spots. It is to invite serious lacunae in one's theology. But we cannot stop here and build a temple. We may build only a tent, and when our reflection is finished, we must pull the tent down and move on.[1]

Reflection upon the person and work of the Holy Spirit reveals that he is the executive of the Godhead. There is no biblical doctrine of a metaphysical or ontological connection between Creator and creation, between Maker and creature. *The connection is direct;* it is made by the Holy Spirit, the divine executive. He touches the creation and the creature directly. Yet in this touching, in this work as executive, he does not originate the plans of his action, but he executes the plans of others. He acts with reference to something *beyond* himself. He is one who witnesses (John 15:26), and therefore the content of this witness exists "outside" himself. He is the gift of the Father to the Son, and of the Son to the disciples; so he carries out the intentions of another.

The Holy Spirit thus displaces all supposed ontological connections between God and man. He replaces totally and completely all metaphysical connective tissue which philosophers and theologians have dreamed of to connect God and man. The contact is direct, and it is the contact of the executive of the Trinity.

The *testimonium* is a work of this person. It is the work of an executive who is making concrete and real the plans of the Father and the Son in the believer. There is no mediating angel, no mediating principle, no ontological or metaphysical something; it is the *direct* act of God the Spirit. It is the touch of the divine Spirit upon the human spirit. This does not exhaust the work of the Spirit upon man; but it is certainly one of his most significant actions. Therefore the *testimonium* must be seen as the *testimonium* of the Holy Spirit of the divine Trinity. It must be seen as an act which in every way is in keeping with the work of the Holy Spirit. He is the executive of the Trinity, so the *testimonium* is one of his executive acts. The *testimonium* is the touch of the Holy

---

1 And here is the standard objection of historic Christianity and Reformed theology, to all forms of enthusiasm, fanaticism, and Pentecostalism. They build a temple where Scripture permits only a tent.

Spirit upon man's spirit; not the only touch, but an important one.[2]

Section 5: The testimonium *and the doctrine of revelation*

In simplest definition, revelation is God making himself known, and this "knowing" is a spiritual knowing. The Eternal Spirit creates a bridge from his infinitude to the finitude of man; he imparts to man a knowledge of himself, and through that knowledge creates a fellowship with the creature. Whether man is sinless or sinful, in paradise or wandering on the face of the earth, he can know God only as God makes himself known to him.

In the course of divine revelation, the revelation reveals its own structure. The speaker is God the Father, whom the revelation exhibits as the Sovereign One of the Trinity, the author, originator, and Lord of all. What the speaker says, he says through his Son, for the Son is the mediator of the Trinity. In the Son the Godhead steps out into the open. It is the Son who is the Logos — the uttered Speech of God. It is the Son who is the incarnate God. His person is the mirror of the divine knowledge. He is the mediator and content of revelation. What the Son mediates is realized within the creature by the executive of the Trinity, the Holy Spirit. He touches the creature so that revelation may come into his orbit, into his consciousness, and into his hands.

The actual production of revelation as knowledge, as tradition, as Scripture, and as illumination is, then, the work of the Holy Spirit. What the Father speaks the Son mediates, and what the Son mediates is actually spoken into the ear by the Holy Spirit. As the one who touches the creature, he has access to the inner ear and the inner eye to give a word and a vision. How appropriate it is, then, to read in Scripture: "Well spake the Spirit through the mouth of the prophet." What the prophet speaks and what the prophet writes is accomplished by virtue of the indwelling and inward revealing

---

2 Cf. Abraham Kuyper, *The Work of the Holy Spirit*, as the most reflective and profound treatment of these subjects.

Holy Spirit. Thereby the human race actually hears and reads the revelation of God.

This revelation is not revelation for the prophet or for the apostle as an individual. Krusche has shown that Calvin's phrase "dictation of the Spirit" did not refer to the mode of revelation, but to the fact that a prophet or apostle did not speak of himself, nor about his own knowledge, nor for his own gain, *but as a public servant of God*.[3] The prophets and apostles were God's secretaries, God's notaries, God's amanuenses, in the sense that they were God's public servants in making known to Israel, the Church, and humanity his holy will. Therefore the prophets and apostles were also *preachers*. In preaching, the inner revelation of the Spirit becomes the public property God intended it to be. The work of the Spirit must extend, then, to *preaching;* and since this preaching was decreed to be put in a permanent form it was *written*, which must also be the work of the Spirit. In preaching and in writing the divine revelation becomes public domain, as God had intended. There exists, then, a chain of revelation which starts with the infinite God in his infinitude, passes through the mediators whom he employs, and ends finally in a document, Sacred Scripture.

Calvin wrote: "For we cannot with propriety say, there is any knowledge of God where there is no religion or piety. . . . For . . . our mind cannot conceive of God, without ascribing some worship to him" (I,ii,1). This is substantially scriptural. The knowledge of God intends a fellowship and communion of God with man. Knowledge of God merely as theological information is unknown to Scripture. The knowledge of God is *always* the instrument of God to create worship and fellowship within the creature. This does not imply a subjectivistic interpretation of revelation. Revelation comes before we were born, and it shall come after we depart. It comes whether we consent to it or not: Christ died when we were *sinners, helpless,* and *enemies* — this shows how little revelation is asked for and expected by man (cf. Rom. 5:6-10).

---

3 *Das Wirken des Heiligen Geistes nach Calvin,* pp. 167ff. "The categorical imperative of Apostles and Prophets is: to say nothing peculiarly their own" (p. 170).

Therefore when revelation comes, it must come in such a manner that fellowship and worship are created. This, too, is the work of the Spirit and is the correlate to revelation as such. The prophet and apostle not only hear the word of revelation, but they are enabled by the Spirit to recognize it as the divine Word; and as this Word is preached and read, there must be the work of the Spirit in the hearers and readers if revelation is to be grasped as revelation, and if communion and worship are to become realities. Upon the objective truth of revelation must fall the subjective light of the Holy Spirit's illumination. The disciples heard the words of Jesus (Luke 24) and their minds grasped the propositions and their meanings; but at the same time a movement started, not from their ears but from their spirits, and as their ears heard, their hearts burned within them. It is the Spirit who makes the heart burn as the Word is heard. *Thus revelation always comes in this double structure —* the inner and the outer, the objective and the subjective, the hearing ear and the burning heart, the given Word from the speaker and the worship and communion of the hearer.

The *testimonium* must be seen in the light of the double structure of revelation. The *testimonium* is an integral part of this double structure. The *testimonium* exists only by virtue of the objective revelation. The *testimonium* disturbs both ecclesiastical authoritarianism and autonomous philosophy, and so it is branded by both as subjectivism. But the *testimonium* lives only by virtue of the previously existing objective revelation. It presupposes the existent truth of God. It presumes a knowledge of God as tradition (patriarchs), as the written Word, or as the remembered Word (the disciples). The *testimonium* is the inner side, the under side of revelation.

The *testimonium* presumes the mediator, Jesus Christ, and his work. It presumes his mediatorial work in revelation (Heb. 1:1-2). All the law and the prophets speak of him. There can be no *testimonium* until there is the accomplished work of the mediator in his revelation. Both the work of Christ and the *testimonium* are directed toward the sinner. The *testimonium* must presume, then, the saving and revealing work of the Savior. In fact,

its content is the gospel. The *testimonium* thus presumes
both salvation and revelation — even in the Old Testament, where Christ is seen in prospect.

In Christ God is revealed in a person; in Scripture God
is revealed by the medium of truth. The apprehension
of salvation is possible only by the work of the Spirit,
and therefore the apprehension of Christ by the sinner is
possible only by the inner work of the Spirit. Christ is
apprehended only in the illumination granted to men by
the Holy Spirit. And the *testimonium* is (in part) this
work of the Spirit enabling the sinner to see Christ as
the Son of God and as his Savior. Insofar as the truth
of Christ is preserved for us in Scripture, it is through
the Scripture that the mind is illuminated to see the
Savior. Thus the *testimonium* is the inner side of revelation, whether the revelation be emphasized on the one
hand as the person of God's Son, or on the other hand as
the written record of God's Son, Holy Scripture. The
testimonium is part of the total organism of revelation;
an impressive segment of the total structure of revelation; an important thread in the larger fabric of revelation. Therefore, we will understand the *testimonium*
properly only if we properly relate it to the total organism of revelation.

Section 6: *The* testimonium *and redemption*

It has been our intention to show that the *testimonium*
is no single item to be inspected in isolation. It is part
of the total schema of Christian theology, as we have
attempted to illustrate in the previous section by discuss-
ing its relationship to revelation. The *testimonium* has
a relationship similarly to redemption.

A witness presupposes that of which the witness
speaks; namely, a content, an object, an event. Redemption
and revelation are the presuppositions of the *testimonium*.
Revelation and redemption are two streams which run
side by side. Redemption is the total activity of God in
bringing man back from the estrangement of sin to sonship and fellowship. Although it comes to a climax in
the person and work of Christ, it includes the totality of
God's acts for man's salvation. In this sense revelation

is part of redemption, for it is one of God's saving actions for man. But revelation is a special sort of redeeming act, for it centers upon the *knowledge of God*. For example, in the exodus from Egypt we have several great acts of God. But the meaning and significance of these acts must be known or else Moses and the Israelites would have no real notion of what was taking place. Therefore, with these great acts of God goes a great revelation of God. With the incarnation of God in Christ we have the great body of revelation spoken by Christ, and then the reflective revelation given through the apostles. With the action of God there must go the revelation of God. When God acts for man, he does not keep his action a mystery but reveals his intention to man, giving him the meaning of the act.

In the New Testament the climax of the saving and revealing action of God is the one person, Jesus Christ. He is at the same time God's supreme revelation and his supreme act of salvation. He is *Logos* and *Savior;* the *Light* of the world and the *Lamb* which takes away the sin of the world. Just as the *testimonium* is related to the inner side of revelation, so it is related to redemption. Just as the *testimonium* cannot exist without revelation, so it cannot exist without redemption. Revelation is the vessel and redemption is the content; and so if the *testimonium* is related to one, it is related to the other. This content is Jesus Christ and his gospel, and therefore the *testimonium* presumes the saving acts of God in Christ. It presumes the entire gamut of acts from the incarnation to the session of Christ at the right hand of God. Just as the *testimonium* must be drawn into the larger circle of revelation, it must be drawn into the larger circle of redemption.

When Calvin thought of the Scripture as such and the *testimonium,* he emphasized the majesty of Scripture; when he thought of the content of Scripture, he emphasized Jesus Christ and his gospel. One of the tensions within the doctrine of the *testimonium* is to make both of these emphases without splitting the witness in two. The New Testament teaches both of these emphases (as we expect to show) and we must do our best to relate them properly.

Section 7: *The* testimonium *and biblical psychology*

There is no formal psychology in the New Testament. The writers use the terms at hand to express their meanings, and they employ these terms with a flexibility common to all non-technical literature. Nevertheless, the writers wished to convey definite religious truth when they employed psychological terms, and it is this which we intend to explore. Not psychology as such, but a description of man in relation to God, is the writers' real interest. They describe an extraordinary relationship in ordinary terms.

Both the Jews and Greeks, along with most peoples of the earth, use the eye and ear as metaphors for the mind. And so we find in Scripture that three levels of meaning may be distinguished. At the first level, the eye and ear are physical organs. At the second level, they are organs of the soul, where they act as instruments of cognition. But there is also a third level where we read of *spiritual* (*pneumatikōs*) eyes and ears. According to Scripture it is possible to see and hear with the senses, and to see and hear with the mind, while at the same time one does not see or hear with the spirit. This is the only conceivable explanation of Matthew 13:13-15 and Mark 8:18.

The third level of meaning is illustrated by such expressions as the eyes of the understanding (Eph. 1:18), seeing God (Matt. 5:8, I John 3:6), seeing the kingdom of God (John 3:3), and spiritual hearing (John 5:24, John 10:3, Rom. 10:17). The Scriptures also speak of such entities as the *heart,* the *soul,* the *spirit,* and (with several different words) the *mind,* which function as the locus of spiritual activities. It also mentions the products of the actions of the mind or heart, such as thoughts, meditations, and words. We may summarize as follows: *there is an inward power, or ability, or faculty in man which is deeper than the ordinary cognitive powers.* That is why Scripture can speak of a hearing which does not hear, and a seeing which does not see. It is this inward power or ability which, when sound and whole, has *an intuitive power for recognizing God and his truth.* This does not mean that we can chart man's inner life, or that we can formulate two psychologies (one for ordinary powers, one for spiritual powers), or that by sheer introspection or by the examination of our experience we can isolate one from the other in our own selves. Like Augustine's city of God and city of man, the two lie confusedly together. But the *testimonium* requires that this distinction be drawn.

That there is a spiritual perception deeper than ordinary cognition is substantiated by what the revelation says of the impairment of this perception. Ears can become dull (Matt. 13:15); eyes may be darkened (Rom. 11:10); minds can be darkened (Rom. 1:21); the heart can be hard and impenitent (Rom. 2:5). There can be seeing without seeing and hearing without hearing (Matt. 13:13-15). On the other hand, we have expressions which speak of the recovery of this power, such as "having the eyes of your hearts enlightened" (Eph. 1:18); the pure in heart seeing God (Matt. 5:8); the heart being opened (Acts 16:14) or being circumcised (Rom. 2:29) or having the veil removed (II Cor. 3:15ff.); spiritual understanding (Col. 1:9); the gift of understanding to know Christ (I John 5:20); and hearing the voice of the Son of God (John 10:3). Paul speaks of spiritual people discerning spiritual things (I Cor. 2:13).

Thus when the natural or unregenerate man considers spiritual things, they appear to him as foolish (I Cor. 1:18, I Cor. 2:14), and a stumblingblock (I Cor. 1:23). But the same matters appear to the man whose spiritual perception has been restored as "the power of God" (I Cor. 1:18); "the wisdom of God" (1:24); "a secret and hidden wisdom of God" (2:7); and as "the mind of Christ" (2:16).

We are further driven to the conclusion that this spiritual perceptivity was part of the *imago Dei*. Levels of perception exist now among men. The cultured person enjoys a concert which bores the farmer; the clever person sees the point of a barb, or the force of a satire, or the meaning of an illustration which eludes the ordinary person; the sensitive moral person sees the ethical issue in a situation which escapes the brutal man. The Scriptures also see man in depth. Man does have "eyes of the heart" and these "eyes of the heart" must have been clear and unclouded in the day of man's creation. There are eyes which see pictures and landscapes; there are eyes which see relationships among concepts and sentences —

brilliant, logical, analytical eyes; there are eyes which
see beauty; there are eyes which see the sublime in human
experience or in nature; there are eyes which see the
finer moral points of our common life; *and there are eyes
that see God!*

Certainly such a doctrine of spiritual perceptivity does
not please those philosophers who want *all* the checkers
on the board so that all may see them; the psychologist
is equally unhappy because he wishes no arcana into which
he is forbidden entrance; and the logician is more than
unhappy, to say the least, for from his perspective this
doctrine appears like special pleading. But the strong
difference in consciousness between belief and unbelief,
between faith and doubt, between obedience and disobedi-
ence is a *sign* (though not a proof) that such a spiritual
perceptivity exists. There are *blessed eyes* which see, and
blessed ears which hear (Matt. 13:16).

The *testimonium* presumes this inward power, this inward faculty which can see God, hear the voice of God,
understand the truth of God, recognize the revelation of
God, and perceive the promises of God. It presupposes
that this power is now crippled and perverse so that the
ear is dull, the eye dim, and the heart fat with insensi-
tivity.

The *testimonium* presupposes that this power can be
restored. Eyes can be opened; hearts can be made tender;
ears can be unplugged; and minds can be enlightened. In
this *restoration* no new thing is added; no new power
created; and no extra spirit given. Rather, a damaged
state of a native power is restored, not to perfection, but
to such a state that it can perceive the truth of God as
it is in itself, the truth of God.[4]

4 Krusche accuses Warfield of stating that in the *testimonium*
a new sense is literally created to enable the believer to perceive
Scripture as the word of God (*Das Wirken des Heiligen Geistes nach
Calvin*, p. 206). Now Warfield at times speaks very strongly in
this matter and almost unguardedly. But in the earlier part of
his essay on Calvin's knowledge of God, he makes it clear that this
"new sense" is not a new creation but a restoration. He specifically
states: "What the operation of the Spirit on the heart does, then,
is to implant, *or rather to restore*, a spiritual sense in the soul by
which God is recognized in his Word" (*Calvin and Augustine*, p.
33). Italics are mine.

Section 8: *The* testimonium *and the Greek language*

The Latin word *testimonium* and the English word "witness" are both interrelated with the Greek *martys*, to which we now turn. The items below are selected from Strathmann's excellent article.[5]

The origin of "witness" is found in legal life and practice. When a person is called a witness, this signifies that he possesses information from his own personal experience by which he can establish the fact or facts of the case. When the word refers to evidence as such, it refers to anything which may be appealed to in order to determine the facts of the case. However, the word and its derivatives, while maintaining a firm connection with legal practice, were extended far beyond this limit.

In the act of witnessing, an objective event of some kind is always presumed. The witness and his testimony possess integrity only when the event in question actually occurred. Otherwise there is false witnessing.

In Aristotle a very significant addition to the meaning of the word was made. Not only is there witnessing in the primary sense of establishing the facts of a case, but also in a second sense in which the witness expresses an opinion and seeks to persuade others to believe as he does. The witness not only states facts as such, but he is convinced of the truthfulness of these matters. Such a persuasive witness, according to Aristotle, is primarily concerned with ethical matters and things of the future. Strathmann writes of these two meanings of witnessing: "In the first instance it deals with the mediation of observable, external facts, be it about an event or condition; in the second, on the contrary, it deals with ethical judgments, and therefore about assertions of ethical convictions, or generally expressed, about opinions. There, on the one hand, assertions will be made about objective events; here, personal convictions are expressed. There it deals with questions if something is real or has existed; here, if something is true according to the opinion of the asserter, and is therefore valid."[6]

5 *"martys, et al.," Theologisches Wörterbuch zum Neuen Testament,* IV, 477-520.

6 *Ibid.,* p. 481.

In the Septuagint another interesting facet is added to the meaning of witnessing: God becomes the subject of witnessing. "For the use of the word *martyrion* in the LXX is accordingly, so far as it goes beyond the secular use, very significant, in that Jahwe himself is the subject of the *martyrein* contained in the *martyrion*. This *martyrein* has been accomplished in the revelation which came through Moses. Its content was the commandments. The complete attachment of the word *martryion* and its plural *martyria* for the self-witnessing of God in the Mosaic giving of the law is of a highest significance for the construction of the Old Testament doctrine of the name of God."[7] Strathmann makes much of Isaiah 43:1-13 and 44:7-11 as forming the basis of the biblical doctrine of religious knowledge and religious certainty. Through God's acts of redemption and revelation Israel had become God's witness to the nations. But the content of the witness is not an objective something which can be known outside of faith; rather, it is known only in faith. It is not capable of rational verification or proof, but can only be something witnessed to; and can be received and known only by those who hear in faith.[8]

We may sum up our discussion at this point as follows: (i) All witnessing is based on the experience of the witness with reference to the order of facts involved. If there is no such reality, the witness is a liar. (ii) From the reporting of facts emerges the second phase of witnessing, namely, the stating of one's opinions (*Ansichten*) as true. The persuasive note enters. And (iii) in the Old Testament, witnessing emerges in a religious context. The Israelites are witnesses to the nations of the deeds of revelation and redemption done by the Lord God.

Turning to the New Testament we find the following matters relevant to our discussion: (i) God is called a witness. He witnesses to the truth of the gospel as preached by the disciples by giving them signs and wonders (Acts 14:3, Heb. 2:4). He witnessed to the true faith of the Gentiles by giving them the Holy Spirit in

7 *Ibid.*, p. 489.
8 *Ibid.*, p. 487.

a remarkable way (Acts 15:8). And he witnesses to
his Son (I John 5:9), and the eternal life which is ours
in his Son (v. 11). (ii) The Holy Spirit is a witness (not
here in the sense of the *testimonium*). He witnesses with
the apostles about the resurrection of Christ (John
15:26); he witnesses particularly to Christ (John 15:
26); he witnesses about the Old Testament Scriptures
(Heb. 10:15); he witnesses about the sufferings of Christ
in the prophets (I Peter 1:11); and then in the sense of
the *testimonium* in verses we shall subsequently discuss.
(iii) The Son is a witness. He is the witness of the revelation of God (Rev. 1:1-2); of a noble witness before
Pilate (I Tim. 6:13); and in numerous passages in John's
gospel he bears witness to the Father. (iv) There is a
fulness of references about the witnessing of the apostles.
Basically their witness is about the life, teachings, death,
resurrection, and ascension of Jesus Christ. They were
divinely called and divinely appointed to this task. In a
wider sense Paul is called a witness (Acts 22:15); and
Stephen is called "thy witness." Strathmann maintains
that the notion of a martyr as one who dies for his faith
is not contained in the New Testament. However, the
beginning is to be found in Jesus Christ as the Crucified
One and in Stephen's death.

CHAPTER III

THE *TESTIMONIUM* AND THE TESTIMONY OF SCRIPTURE

Section 9: The teaching of the Scriptures

To say that the doctrine of the inner witness of the Holy Spirit is based upon one or two passages of Scripture is very misleading. The *testimonium* is an expression employed because of its historical significance. There are a number of biblical passages which interlock with this doctrine on several sides. We concern ourselves in this chapter with a survey of the biblical materials.

I. *Some passages of Scripture attribute the enlightenment of the believer to an act of God the Father.* That God should also be engaged in the action of enlightenment comes as no surprise. It is typical of the New Testament to assign various functions and actions in salvation and sanctification to the members of the Trinity severally. This is a reflection of the riches we have in the doctrine of the Trinity. In two very important passages, which remarkably parallel each other, illumination is attributed to God the Father.

When Peter made his famous confession that this man, Jesus, is the Christ, the Son of the living God (Matt. 16:16), Jesus said that it was not flesh and blood which *revealed* this to Peter but "my Father who is in heaven" (v. 17). Peter, pointing in speech to the man before him, affirmed that this Jewish person was the Christ, the Son of the living God. By use of the word "Messiah" he indicated that this was the one of whom the prophets spoke, the King of Israel, the prophet greater than Moses, the founder of the Kingdom of God, the sum and end of the Old Testament revelation. And when he called him the Son of the living God, he asserted Christ's divinity.[1]

1 The title, the Son of God, "describes His divine status." Vincent Taylor, *The Names of Jesus*, p. 52.

Our Lord said that this confession sprang from no ordinary, no human power of insight. It was not a delivery of Peter's senses nor of his powers of reason. Everything which met the eye or stirred the mind could be equivocated. By stating that the confession was the result of the illuminating work of the Father, Jesus placed it beyond the possible deceit of the eye or the equivocation of the mind. This confession was a statement of revelation, namely, that Jesus is the Christ and the Son of God; it was made by an inward revelation, a *testimonium*. This confession, and the certainty that accompanied it, was the product of the inward revealing act of God the Father and is a reflection of that total New Testament doctrine of illumination.

It is remarkable how II Corinthians 4:3-6 parallels Peter's confession. Peter, who was only flesh and blood, could not know the mystery of God manifest in the flesh without the revelatory action of the Father. Besides the incomprehensibility of this act for flesh and blood, there is another hindrance, the blinding power of sin and Satan. Paul preached "Jesus Christ as Lord" (v. 5). But the god of this world has blinded the eyes of men and this truth does not shine into their hearts. Nevertheless, the god of this world does not have the last word! The almighty Creator, gazing over the eternal bank of gloomy darkness, brought radiant light by the word of his mouth. And if he could by his speaking send shafts of light beaming into the deep recesses of his great creation, how easily can he speak again: not to the darkness of creation, but to the darkness of sin; not to send out physical light but spiritual light, "the light of the gospel of the glory of Christ." Not into the darkness of the creation, but "in our hearts."

When our minds are blinded by the god of this world, everything we read in the New Testament may be equivocated, e.g., "we are not sure of the Greek," "there is a parallel in the mystery cults to this," "this is a piece of Judean tradition," "this is but Paul's imagination," or, "this is a later churchly interpolation." Then, in the midst of our equivocations, God speaks: Let there be light! Immediately this creaturely equivocation ceases; unbelief burns itself out in a moment; and there before the eyes of our hearts stands Jesus Christ giving the light of the knowledge of the glory of God on his blessed face (v. 6).

The *testimonium,* therefore, begins with the Father. So much is it his originative act that the Scriptures may relate it as if there were no Holy Spirit. And yet it is so much the Spirit's act that it can be related without mention of the Father. But here is the great anchorage of this doctrine: that God the Father is almighty, with power to speak into the darkness of the human heart with the radiant light of the gospel. In both Matthew 16 and II Corinthians 4 the light of revelation falls on the face of Jesus Christ.

II. A second group of passages indicates that *as a result of God's illuminatory activity the Christian possesses the Word of God in himself.* "Of his own will he brought us forth by the word of truth," writes James (1:18). God is the sovereign actor, and the new birth is the wonderful result. But the instrument of the divine begetting is the word of truth (the word that by its nature is true). The verb "brought" is associated in other contexts with the work of a midwife. God brings his children into spiritual existence (or birth) by the instrument of the gospel, and thus the gospel is stamped indelibly into their new natures. There is no regeneration without the impressing of the gospel upon the soul. Thus the gospel becomes sealed within the soul and John can write of the Word of God *being in us* (I John 1:10, 2:14).

The mark of the unbeliever is that the Word of God is not in him. This *in him* must be taken strictly. It cannot mean merely in his mind as a matter of memory. Unregenerate men have memories of the gospel. It must mean *in him* in a real and abiding manner so that it controls thought and action. In fact, it must be such a powerful indwelling that it establishes the difference between those who are regenerate and those who are not. If such evidence is lacking, we may question the work of grace in the heart. Thus the illuminating work of the Father is no simple flash of light. This light is truth and we are not only enabled to see the truth as truth, but the truth is impressed upon the soul. We are begotten by the truth, and the truth becomes a powerful resident of the soul. The light not only shines upon the soul but it brands its own image upon it. In the words of Martin Luther: "Since these promises of God are holy, true, righteous, free, and peaceful words, full of goodness, the soul which clings to them with a firm faith will be so closely united with them and altogether absorbed by them that it not only will share in all their power but will be saturated and intoxicated by them. If a touch of Christ healed, how much more will this most tender spiritual touch, this absorbing WORD of God, communicate to the soul all things that belong to the Word."[2]

III. *Another group of passages attributes enlightenment to the Son.* This too comes as no surprise, especially after the insights gained from the doctrine of the Trinity. It is the Father who originates this action, and it is the Son who mediates it. The great passage which speaks of the mediatorial work of the Son of God in the enlightenment of the heart with a true knowledge of God is Matthew 11:27, "All things have been delivered to me by my Father." The expression "my Father" is an intra-trinitarian expression. The totality of the knowledge of God necessary for our salvation has been delivered to the Son. He is the mediator. He alone knows the Father since he is the Son in the bosom of the Father (John 1:18), and therefore can "exegete" (Greek *eksēgēsato*) the Father. Thus our Lord did not blaspheme when he made the remarkable statement that "He who believes in me, believes . . . in him who sent me. And he who sees me sees him who sent me" (John 12:44-45).

Sinners are introduced to the Father only as they are introduced to the Father by the Son. The Son must choose to *reveal* the Father. Only in a *revelation* can the Father be known, and this *revelation* must be mediated. It is God who speaks to overcome our darkness, and it is the Father who reveals to Peter the person of his Son; but it is mediated speaking and revealing by the Son. Thus, with Calvin, we are confined to a christologically mediated knowledge of God (III,ii,1). The Son not only mediates salvation, he also mediates the knowl-

2 "The Freedom of a Christian," *Luther's Works*, XXXI, 349.

edge of God. He who learns of the Father will also "learn from me" (v. 29).

An interesting parallel to this passage is Galatians 1:16, where Paul writes, "God revealed his Son in me." It is God who speaks, and what he says is "Jesus Christ." Unless God spoke these words, we would never hear them. It is the Father who reveals the Son, yet it is the Son who reveals the Father. Thus we may say with equal propriety: "The Father reveals the Son," and, "The Son reveals the Father."

John 10 parallels Matthew 11:27, for it speaks of sheep *hearing* the voice of the shepherd (10:3, 4, 16, 27 and compare John 8:37, 47). What is this hearing? Certainly not of the mere sounds of the words, and certainly not the registering of the meaning of the words in the consciousness. It can only refer to the deeper, spiritual hearing previously discussed. It can only mean that the shepherd has so worked inwardly, spiritually, in an act of revelation and illumination, that his voice is distinguished from all other voices. Here is the *hearing of the voice* that must be combined with that regenerative power which enables a voice to be heard, and an illuminating power which enables the voice to be heard as the Word of God, and a persuasive power which calls forth such an assent that obedience follows. *They hear and follow!* The hearing of the sheep is but a metaphor for the Father who speaks and the light that shines, and the Son who mediates, making the Father known.

In its own way the most remarkable verse upon this subject is I John 5:20; "And we know that the Son of God has come and has given us an understanding, to know him who is true; and we are in him who is true, in his Son Jesus Christ. This is the true God and eternal life." This is Christianity in its radical doctrine of revelation, its radical christology, and its radical soteriology. There is no knowledge of God without revelation, and there is no knowledge of God that is not christological, and there is no salvation without this knowledge of God and of Christ.

The person here is no less than God the Son. A christological assertion short of this can make no sense of this text. He has come; *the incarnation,* no less. And in this coming he gave us an understanding (*dianoia*). What an utterly profound frustration would come to pass if the great humiliation of the Son of God took place and the human race were unaware of its occurring; and how humanly impossible it would be for Jewish men to single out a particular man as God incarnate. From the divine side and from the human side the only resolution is that the Son of God should give men an understanding of who he is. The *giving of an understanding* is one aspect of the complex of revelation and the *testimonium*. Here is the Father speaking; the Son mediating; the Spirit illuminating. The tenses are also worthy of notice: "the Son of God has come" (*hēkei*) signifies the reality in space and time, as the act of God accomplished; "we know" (*oidamen*) and "he has given" (*dedōken*). These acts are accomplished, finished, completed as expressions of their surety and reality.

Furthermore, this is a saving knowledge of God. We *know* him that is true and this knowing can only be the knowing of salvation. Here is Matthew 11:27 repeated in a different context with different words, but asserting the identical truth: by an act of revelation the Son introduces the Father to believing men, and there arises in the spirits of believing men a christological knowledge of God, and a theocentric knowledge of Jesus Christ. And so intimate is this relationship of the Father with the Son that it is difficult for exegetes to determine whether the last sentence refers to the Father or the Son ("this is the true God and eternal life"). It can be said of either and both in full loyalty to the total knowledge of God and our Lord, Jesus Christ.

IV. *Some passages refer to a great inward saving operation of the Holy Spirit.* The *testimonium*, as we have insisted many times, is part of a larger complex. It must now be considered in the light of the mighty acts of the Holy Spirit of God upon the human soul. There is no better point of beginning than John 3:1ff. Here humanity is described in all its helplessness — it is flesh, utterly weak and helpless flesh. It is sinful flesh, dead in trespasses and sins. Such helpless and sinful flesh cannot enter the kingdom of God nor even see the kingdom of

God. It stands as unworthy and helpless to enter the door, and too blind to see it.

The Spirit is the antithesis to flesh and therefore has the power to overcome the weakness and helplessness of the flesh. It can exert such power upon a man that he comes to a new birth and can *see* and *enter* the kingdom of God. It is the Spirit who gives strength where there is weakness, life where there is death, sight where there is blindness, light where there is darkness. He is the mighty wind of God who can blow through our souls and give us the new birth.

The Spirit moves powerfully, for he is the divine breath; he moves mysteriously because he is invisible as the wind is at night; and he moves efficaciously, for after he moves, we are born again. No person must underestimate the power of God in effecting the new birth. It is a re-creation, a resurrection, and a great transformation. As a mystery it is beyond the touch of psychologists who would investigate it empirically and philosophers who would investigate it analytically.

When Nicodemus asked, "How can this be?" (v. 9), the answer is John 3:16. Here the complete union of the christological and the pneumatological is seen. The new birth only by faith in Jesus Christ; and only in Jesus Christ crucified; and only as effected by the Holy Spirit.

Very closely connected to John 3:1ff. is Matthew 3:11, which tells us that in contrast to John's water baptism there shall be a baptism of the Holy Spirit by Jesus Christ. Just as we are baptized by another, so Christ the divine servant baptizes us with the Holy Spirit. As water baptism was for the remission of sins to mark a moral and spiritual turning point in a man's life, so the baptism of the Spirit marks an even greater turning point. Water touches only the body, but the Holy Spirit touches the heart. The baptism of the Spirit is a baptism of power, of renewal, of the impartation of spiritual life and moral quickening. There is perhaps no stronger language to indicate the character of this inward action of the Spirit upon the soul of man than the picture of the mighty Son of God baptizing with the Holy Spirit.

Paul wrote to the Galatians that their Christian life had begun in the Spirit (3:3). This can only mean the regenerating work of the Holy Spirit. Yet in closest connection with this he places the crucifixion (3:1). This again shows the intimate connection of the cross with regeneration already noted in John 3.

Beginning in the Spirit is set forth in a striking manner in II Corinthians 3:1-3. The law was written by the finger of God upon a stone slate. What more impressive utterance can there be than this? What is more sacred than the finger of God and what is more permanent than stone? Yet the New Testament surpasses the Old. The instrumental finger is replaced by the living Holy Spirit, and the inanimate stone is replaced by the living human person. The ink biting into the material and fixing the message there firmly is the Holy Spirit. Paul seems to imply a double imagery here (in a perfectly fitting way) in which the Holy Spirit is both the stylus and the ink. The message is: *Jesus Christ!*

The *testimonium* is part of this great and powerful inward ministry of the Holy Spirit. This inward ministry is not exhausted by the *testimonium*, but the inward ministry would be incomplete without it. The point needs emphasis here because the *testimonium* is alleged by Roman Catholics and others to imply subjectivism. This is far from the truth. And it must also be seen that the *testimonium* is not the religious experience of Protestant liberalism. Nor can we permit the philosopher to engage us in any sort of argument which presupposes the surrendering of the *testimonium* for purposes of debate.

V. *A number of passages attribute the certainty of Christian consciousness in the divinity of the faith to an inward action of the Holy Spirit.* The Christian does have a *full persuasion* of the truth of the gospel (*plērophoria*, full assurance, conviction, certainty, as in Col. 2:2 and I Thess. 1:5). This *plērophoria* is the product of the inward working of the Holy Spirit. Paul puts in closest conjunction the operation of the Spirit and the truth of the gospel (II Thess. 2:13). On God's side we are saved by God himself, but Paul informs us that the two means employed are the sanctifying action of the Holy Spirit and belief in the truth. Thus the action of the Spirit is one side, and belief in the truth is the other side.

In I Corinthians 12:3 Paul writes that no man can say that Jesus is Lord unless he is enabled by the Holy Spirit. Here is the shortest of creeds, "Jesus is Lord," yet nonetheless it is so impressive that it can be confessed (not merely recited) only by the inward impulse of the Holy Spirit. Certainly with an impulse such as this there also comes the Christian certainty and conviction of the truth.

We are, according to II Corinthians 1:22, sealed by the Holy Spirit. This sealing contains an eschatological note.[3] We are sealed *for* something, and Paul states that this something is the day of redemption (Eph. 4:30). But what is the meaning of this seal? Certainly in its first dimension it is an act of God as real as the cross and resurrection, as justification and atonement, and therefore is to be given its full weight of importance. It is a sealing to ourselves of the reality, truthfulness, purposes, and divinity of the gospel. It is both an invisible sealing by God upon the heart, and yet a sealing in our own consciousness as the truth of the gospel is impressed upon it. It therefore witnesses to the truth that our conviction of the reality and truthfulness of the Christian faith is brought to us and imparted to us by the Holy Spirit in his sealing action.

The two classical passages of the *testimonium* are Galatians 4:6 ("and because ye are sons, God has sent the Spirit of his Son into our hearts, crying, 'Abba! Father!'"); and Romans 8:15-16 ("For you did not receive the spirit of slavery to fall back into fear, but you have received the spirit of sonship. When we cry, 'Abba! Father!' it is the Spirit himself bearing witness with our spirit that we are children of God").

When we survey these two passages of Scripture, the one great truth which stands out is *that our consciousness of salvation in Jesus Christ is the result of the action of the Holy Spirit.* However, we must start with the ultimate source of this consciousness: it is the Father himself. God has sent his Spirit, and we have received his Spirit. The final and ultimate divinity of this en-

3 Cf. in general N. Q. Hamilton, *The Holy Spirit and Eschatology in Paul.*

tire procedure is certified in the divine sending resulting in a human receiving.

The next observation is the intense *soteriological* aspect of this witness of the Spirit. It is not a witness about religion, or even about Christianity as a religious system, nor about the existence of God, nor to the reality of a plan of salvation in general. Rather, it is a witness to individual participation in salvation; of the divine adoption. The intent of the witness is to bear witness to *our* participation in this redemption. The witness is, then, not associated with the general call of the gospel, but with its *internal hearing*. It is intensely personal without being subjectivistic or individualistic.

Next we notice its *trinitarian* aspect. It is the Father who sends the Spirit; the Spirit is the Spirit of the Son; it is a witness of the saving action of the Father in the Son; and when the believer cries in response to the witness of the Spirit, he cries, "Father." The *testimonium* is trinitarian through and through.

Both the Spirit and the believer *cry*. The Greek word, *kradzōn*, means "to cry, to shriek." These are certainly not audible cries. The word is used, rather, to signify intensity of feeling. The crying speaks of the strength of the impulse of the Holy Spirit and of its intensity. The *testimonium*, when unhindered, is not a weak something; *it is a crying*.

And what is the word we cry but *Father!* This is the revelation our Lord brought about God. This is not wholly a New Testament revelation (Deut. 32:6), but Jesus Christ made it peculiarly the name of God in the New Covenant. It is a name which expresses his relationship to God as the Son of the Father, and our redemption and adoption as God's dear children. We cry "Father" because it indicates that our redemption and adoption is accomplished. Atonement, resurrection, justification by faith, all anticipate the birth-cry of the newborn infant, "Father." Until there is that cry, the entire heavenly machinery has not fulfilled its intention. That is why the particular content of the witness of the Spirit is the one word, *Father*, which is significantly also the Gethsemane cry (Mark 14:36).

It is interesting that in Galatians 4:6 it is the Spirit who

cries, "Father," and in Romans 8:15-16 it is the believer!
This is harmonized in Paul's expression in Romans 8:16,
summartureo — to bear witness with, or, to establish
before. The locus of the *testimonium* is the human spirit,
and both the divine Spirit and the human spirit cry the
same thing, *Father*. These are not two cries but one cry.
They are like two forks of the same pitch which vibrate
sympathetically and harmoniously together. We *both* cry;
we *both* cry *Father* — it is the same cry, the same content, to the same God.[4]

The place of the crying is the human spirit or heart.
The word *our* (or *your*) is immensely important. Although this witness is individual, it has a corporate dimension. It is the common witness of God's sons. So
the apostle does not say pietistically or individualistically
my spirit or *my* heart. The *testimonium* is at the very
center of our being, where nothing can be deeper. Only
the Spirit can touch us here — touch us really, profoundly,
permanently. Yet in the profundity of this witness its
common dimension must not be forgotten.

Because it is in the heart or spirit, it has been called a
secret witness or an inner witness. It is common to all
Christians but not to all men. It is inner and therefore
not a datum available to psychologists or philosophers.
There is a great objectivity here and at the same time a
real subjectivity. All Christians have sympathetic rapport with those fellow Christians who have the same
witness in their hearts. Yet this witness can in no sense
be made a public object. Therefore most philosophers
and psychologists will always suspect its integrity, which
need cause Christians no concern. If it is true that only
the pure in heart can see God, then there is nothing more
to say except that spiritual realities must be spiritually
discerned.

The most extensive discussion of the work of the Spirit

---

4 Cf. Strathmann, *summartureo, et al., Theologisches Wörterbuch zum Neuen Testament*, IV, 514-517. The word has had two
meanings: to witness with (*mitbezeugen*), and, to confirm (*bestä-
tigen*). Strathmann takes it in the second sense in Rom. 8:16. If
it is taken in the first sense (strongly) it would give the human
spirit power to say "Father" without the Holy Spirit, which is not
in keeping with Paul's basic teaching.

with respect to revelation and illumination is contained in I Corinthians 2. The subject matter is the "testimony of God," or "Jesus Christ and him crucified," or "my message," or "a secret, and hidden wisdom of God." This gospel, this testimony of God, does not find entrance into the human mind by reason of the oratorical powers of the preacher but by the "demonstration of the Spirit and power" (v. 4). If a man were persuaded by man, i.e., by persuasive oratorical power, then faith would rest in the wisdom of man and not in the power of God. If the mind is persuaded by the power of the Holy Spirit, then its faith rests in the power and authority of God.

This testimony of God, as Paul calls the gospel, appears foolish to the unregenerate mind, but to the regenerate mind it is the wisdom of God. The testimony of God is not known to the natural man because he is ignorant in his sin. The natural man does not know the "secret and hidden wisdom of God." But God in a great act of revelation has declared his secret and hidden wisdom, which is the gospel.

Those great realities of revelation are revealed to us by God through the Holy Spirit (v. 10). We note here: (i) the originator of the objective revelation is God, and therefore this objective revelation exists in its own right prior to any man's awareness of it; (ii) the one who reveals this revelation in our hearts is God, the author, dispenser, and governor of this inward revelation; (iii) the objective revelation, the testimony of God, is revealed in our hearts *directly* by the Holy Spirit, who is the actual effector, the actual executive of that inward illumination which finds its originating impulse in God the Father. Here we have the *testimonium* in its great structure as revelation. With the objective revelation (the testimony of God) there is the inward revelation (the *testimonium*). God speaks his word by prophet and apostle; he speaks it again in our hearts by the Holy Spirit. He *repeats* it by the Holy Spirit. As Calvin maintained, the same Spirit which "spake by the mouths of the prophets" must "penetrate into our hearts" and thus, as it were, *repeat* the message to us, convincing us of its divine origin (I,vii,4).

Paul is very explicit that the inward illumination of the objective revelation is the work of the Holy Spirit.

It is the Spirit who knows the depths of God. Therefore
if any man will ever know the mind of God (or of Christ,
v. 16), he can know it only by an act of the Holy Spirit.
There is no other access to the depths of God; we are
confined to a revelational knowledge of God given objectively through the Holy Spirit, and mediated personally
by the illumination of the same Spirit. Only in this way
can a man comprehend the thoughts of God (cf. v. 11).

At this point Paul informs us that the Christian has
the Holy Spirit. *The Spirit establishes the direct connection from the mind of God to the mind of the Christian.*
Because Christians have the Holy Spirit, they have the
possibility established whereby they can know it. And,
having the Spirit, Christians do understand the revelation of God. *Christians do understand.* The Spirit illuminates the objective revelation with his inward operation.   What Paul discussed soteriologically in Romans
8:15-16 and in Galatians 4:6 he here discusses from the
perspective of so-called theory of knowledge. It is the
same *testimonium;* it has the same content; and it has
the same structure. We may discuss the *testimonium* and
emphasize it as the knowledge of God; or we may emphasize its soteriological content.

There is a second reason why the unregenerate cannot
know the mind of God. The first is that only the *divine*
Spirit knows the depths of God; the second is that, lacking
the Holy Spirit and possessing a rebellious mind, the unregenerate simply has no grounds for comprehending
God's revelation. It appears to him as foolishness. His
mind is bent in one direction and the revelation of God in
another. The revelation goes so contrary to his religious
and spiritual dispositions that he judges it as foolishness.
The regenerate man knows why the testimony of God appears as foolishness to the unregenerate; but the unregenerate is mystified by the faith of the believer and can only
presume that there is something defective (any appearances of learning or culture being deceptive) in the Christian's rational processes.

Paul concludes his discussion with a remarkable statement: "but we have the mind of Christ" (*noun Christou*).
The inward *testimonium,* the mind of the Lord, and the
mind of Christ are one and the same thing. This shows

two things: (i) that the reality and concreteness of this witness is so strong we can be said to have the *mind of Christ;* and (ii) that the *testimonium* is at the same time soteriological (v. 1), christological (v. 16), pneumatological, and epistemological.

The structure underlying I Corinthians 2 also underlies II Corinthians 3; namely, that with the giving of an objective revelation, there is an accompanying inward revelation enabling man to apprehend the objective revelation as truth. And this inward revelation is the *testimonium.*

The chapter commences with the remarkable picture discussed previously; namely, that the Holy Spirit writes the gospel upon the heart of the Christian so that the reality and the certainty of the Christian faith to the believer is the result of the direct action of the Holy Spirit (vv. 1-3). Paul continues by affirming that this writing of the name of Christ upon the heart of the believer is not the product of his own power, but it occurs in the ministry of his preaching by the enablement of God (vv. 4-6). In this connection he introduces the New Covenant.

The heart of this New Covenant is not a code, a document which is external to the life-impulse of the believer, but it is the Holy Spirit (v. 6). The law (the written code) kills because it arouses sin in the sinful man, and condemns the sin that is aroused (cf. Romans 7). But the New Covenant is just as much *written* as the Old Covenant — for it is first recorded by Jeremiah and repeated in Hebrews 8; and the institutional words are *written* in the Gospels and repeated in I Corinthians 10. The point of contrast is not that one covenant is written and the other is not but one is in some way supported invisibly by the Spirit. *Both* are written covenants! The point of difference is that the Old is *only* written whereas the New is not only written but is also the instrument used in effecting the spiritual illumination of the human heart. The New Covenant is written by the Holy Spirit upon the believing heart and thereby becomes part of the very nature of the regenerate man. As Hebrews cites Jeremiah: "I will put my laws into their minds, and write them on their hearts" (8:10). The New Covenant written in the heart by the Holy Spirit *gives life* (II Cor. 3:6).

The New Covenant is called *the dispensation of the*

Spirit (v. 8), and *the dispensation of righteousness* (v. 9). The writing of the objective revelation in the heart by the Holy Spirit permeates the New Covenant. The written covenant is rewritten in the heart by the Spirit of God. Seen noetically, as illumination, it is the *testimonium;* seen as a spiritual resurrection, as the powerful impartation of spiritual life, it is regeneration. And because the New Covenant is this rich ministry of the Holy Spirit, Paul calls it the dispensation of the Spirit.

Although what Paul says in the last part of II Corinthians 3 refers directly to the Jews, it has an indirect application to all. The Jewish heart is hard (v. 14) and veiled (v. 14). It is impossible for the Jewish mind in this condition to read the Old Covenant and see Jesus Christ in its prophecies. Only as they are *in Christ* can they understand their own Scriptures (v. 14). When the Jew turns to the Lord, the veil is removed (v. 16). The truth of Christ is in the Old Testament whether a Jew reads it there or not. Revelation has occurred. But the mind of the Jew is veiled and hardened and he does not see it as the truth of God. Only in Christ is the veil removed, pulled back by the Lord. But Paul immediately adds: "the Lord is the Spirit" (v. 17). It is only the Spirit who can soften the hard heart and remove the veil so that the believing Jew with "unveiled face [beholds] the glory of the Lord . . . for this comes from the Lord who is the Spirit" (v. 18). And this is but the *testimonium* in another one of its forms.

John is the other New Testament writer who has much to say about the *testimonium,* especially in its noetic aspect. In I John 2 he defines the antichrist as the one who denies that "Jesus is the Christ" (v. 22). The center of the New Testament revelation is, then, that Jesus is the Christ. It is this truth which the antichrist denies and the Christian affirms. The believer has come to this knowledge by an anointing of the Holy One (v. 20). John then adds: *and you know all things.* It is the work of the Holy Spirit which leads the believer into the knowledge of the truth described here as an anointing (*chrisma*). Then in v. 27 he states that this anointing *abides.* The illuminating, persuading ministry of the Holy Spirit is no impulse which decays, no flash of light without duration, no emotional storm which subsides, but a permanent possession of the believer (*menei en hymeis*).

In I John 3:24 the apostle avers that a real Christian keeps the teachings of his Lord and this is the sign that he abides in the Lord, and the Lord abides in him. And the certainty, the persuasion that the Lord abides in us, is given to us by the Spirit who has been given to us by the Lord. The pattern here is interesting: there is the teaching of Christ, which is the objective revelation bound upon every believer and then written in the New Testament; there is the Lord Jesus who *gave* the teaching, and who *sends* the Spirit into the believer, and who himself comes and abides in us; and there is the Spirit in our heart who *bears witness* that the Lord Christ is there too! Here we are led to see again the christological and soteriological aspect of the *testimonium* joined with the noetic aspect.

VI. *Some passages show the unusually strong connection between the Holy Spirit and the word of truth.* Our Lord taught that it is the Spirit who gives life (John 6:63). Man's own powers, "the flesh," cannot give to man a spiritual life. The words which Jesus Christ spoke are spirit and life! The spoken word of Christ (part of which was eventually written) is the truth of God, the objective revelation. And as such it is the fit medium for the work of the Holy Spirit. The Holy Spirit, taking the words of Christ, applies them to the human heart and the result is spiritual life.

The Holy Spirit is called the Spirit of truth (John 14:17). He is the Spirit who is veracious within himself; and in his ministry he ministers the truth. He is the divine teacher; and his textbook is the truth; and his pupils are believers; and his intention is to instill the truth into the human mind in such a way that it appears as the truth, that it is embraced as the truth, and that it powerfully influences thought and conduct. The Holy Spirit will teach the disciples all things (John 14:26). He is sent by the Father in the name of Jesus Christ and his purpose is to teach and to bring to remembrance to the minds of the disciples those things which the Lord taught them. Here in this ministry of the Spirit is the ultimate credibility of the New Testament; here is the sufficient and necessary cause for the writing of the New Testament; here is the authority of the divine Scriptures traced to their executor; and here is the real ground of our own inward certainty of the Christian faith. And the *testimonium* is an integral element in the teaching ministry of the Holy Spirit.

The Spirit witnesses to Christ along with the witness of the disciples (John 15:26-27). The function of a witness is: (i) to bear witness to certain facts known directly to the witness; (ii) to bear this witness with the spirit of persuasion to bring others to the same conviction. The Spirit, as a witness, bears witness to one great reality, Jesus Christ; and he bears a persuasive witness to this great reality. Certainly this is a witnessing to men, and it is not isolated from the witness of the apostles but with them and through them (Heb. 2:4). In his sovereignty he chooses his own ways of witnessing. We may gather some notions of his witnessing by reading the Book of Acts and noticing that, when it is necessary, he will employ the miracle or the unusual; or we may study carefully Paul's writings to see how Paul structures the various works of the Holy Spirit.[5]

The intense christological character of the pneumatology of the New Testament is stated in John 16:14, "He will glorify me." An abstract witness of the Spirit directed towards the divinity of the Scriptures is very contrary to those Scriptures which set forth the Christ-centered character of the *testimonium*.

Paul writes that the gospel comes in word and Spirit (I Thess. 1:5), and this is the simplest statement of the Protestant position. The Word — the divine revelation, the gospel, the person of Christ; and the Spirit — the one who takes this Word and makes it a personal reality to believing sinners. We are reminded of Paul's graphic expression in Ephesians 6:17 — the word of God, which is the sword of the Spirit. There are two hands on the sword: for *we* take the sword, and yet, since it is the sword of the Spirit, *his* hand is also on the hilt. We are not to use this sword by ourselves, on our own authority,

5 Cf. H. Wenland, "Das Wirken des Heiligen Geistes in den Gläubigen nach Paulus," *Theologische Literaturzeitung*, LXXVII (1952), 457-470.

and by our own sovereignty. We are to be completely
sensitive to the pressure of the Spirit's hand in ours.
Unless the Spirit wields the sword, we shall use it to no
avail. And notice the union of Word and Spirit. The
Spirit works only with an organ, an instrument, the
Word; and the Word is efficacious only as the Spirit
wields it. Therefore the Word will find lodgment in the
human heart only as it is lodged there by the Holy Spirit.
And the Holy Spirit leads to faith and to Christ and to
eternal life only as he works with the Holy Scripture.

I John 5:6-12 is a most remarkable passage in connection with the *testimonium*. In v. 5 John mentions Jesus
as the Son of God, and then in v. 6 affirms that the Son
of God came by water and blood. Commentators take
this to mean his baptism and his death. The events of
baptism (water) and the cross (blood) are the brackets
for the public ministry of Christ. At his baptism our
Lord stepped into his public ministry, and at his cross he
stepped out of it. The intervening three years constitute the
public life of the Messiah. Then John adds words which
come unexpectedly: "And the Spirit is witness because
the Spirit is truth" (v. 7). We are thus led to understand the entire public life of Christ as *one* witness; and
the Spirit as the *second* witness. But certainly these
two witnesses are of a different order. One is the witness
of a public life; and the other must mean the *peculiar
meaning* of this life to the spirits of men. John then
states that these three witnesses (the water, the blood,
the Spirit) have the same intent: *that Jesus Christ is the
Son of God who came into the world to give men eternal
life.* The baptism is the beginning of the public life,
the blood is the end, and the Spirit gives the inner witness; all three bear witness to the *intent* of this objective
(i.e., public) life of Christ, namely, to give sinners eternal life. The public life of Christ and the inner witness
of the Spirit are called by John "the testimony of God"
(v. 9). And the testimony of God is greater than any
testimony of man. Therefore if men are prudent and
accept the good and trustworthy testimony of men, how
much more should they accept the testimony of God. The
testimony of God is that testimony he bore of his Son;
his public life from baptism to crucifixion. He who be-

lieves God has the meaning and the intention sealed in his heart by the Holy Spirit, and so he has the witness "within himself" (v. 10). To deny the meaning of the life of Jesus, the public witness of God, is to make God a liar. Those who perceive the divine meaning of the life of Christ receive eternal life, and this is called the witness of God as the obverse side of the public life of Christ. Thus the subjective intention of the life of Jesus, the Son of God, namely, eternal life, stands for the objective life itself.

One other section of Scripture is especially relevant in speaking of Word and Spirit, and that is Revelation 2 and 3. In each of the letters to the seven churches is contained the exhortation for the individual to listen to what the Spirit says to the Church. The Spirit does speak to the Church! But what does he say and how does he say it? Certainly John intended that each letter should be sent to its church, and that this letter contained what the Spirit intended to say to each church. The Spirit would speak in the letter, but only those with an ear to hear would hear what the Spirit was speaking to the Church. The One who gives the ear to hear is the same Spirit who inspired the letter to be written. The objective truth or revelation is heard with spiritual ears opened by the selfsame Spirit who is its author.

VII. *Some passages of Scripture show an interesting reversal of the relationship of Word and Spirit by speaking of a test for spirits by the Word.* This, of course, is a reminder of Calvin's debate with the enthusiasts of his day, who claimed to be guided by the Spirit without the Word. In I Corinthians 12:3 Paul says that no man speaking by the so-called prompting of the Holy Spirit calls Jesus accursed. The spirit which says this is not God's Spirit, for the Word of God reveals Jesus as Lord.

John says that we are not to believe every spirit but we are to test (*dokimadzō*) spirits (I John 4:1-6). The test of the Spirit of God is that he prompts the confession that Jesus Christ is come in the flesh (i.e., the incarnation) ; and the test for antichrist is that the spirit of error (*planē*, a wandering, error, deceit) denies the incarnation. Thus, with Calvin, any confession of faith which does not conform to the New Testament truth is not prompted by the Spirit of God, for the Spirit conforms to the image of himself given in Holy Scripture.

If the Spirit witnesses in the Word, then Word and Spirit form a harmony. This harmony may be destroyed from both sides. Rationalistic intellectualism, which seeks to defend the authority of Scripture apart from the Spirit, is at one end of the log; and enthusiasts and fanatics of whom John and Paul speak are at the other end. We may err about both the Word and the Spirit. When the rationalistic apologist errs about the witness of the Spirit, he must be forcibly reminded of the *testimonium;* and when the fanatic errs doctrinally, he must be reminded forcibly of the Word.

Another matter is very important here, namely, that both John (the incarnation) and Paul ("Jesus is Lord") stress the strong christological character of the *testimonium.* A man may err at every point of systematic theology; but the most dangerous point, spiritually and theologically, at which to err is christology, concerning the blessed person of Jesus Christ our Lord and Savior. That is why the Bible does not give us a list of all possible errors, but speaks to the heart of the *testimonium* — Jesus Christ the Son of God.

CHAPTER IV

THE THEOLOGICAL IMPLICATIONS OF THE *TESTIMONIUM*

To this point we have endeavored to show how the doctrine of the *testimonium* originated, its theological presuppositions, and its scriptural foundation. It will now be our purpose to draw out the theological implications of the *testimonium*.

Section 10: *Word and Spirit*

In the historical section it was noted that the *testimonium* was not in the foreground at the inception of the Reformation. It was implied in the original positions of the Reformers and was eventually formulated by Calvin. But the doctrine of Word and Spirit was developed early in the Reformation,[1] and has not only a temporal priority over the *testimonium*, but also a theological priority. The union of Word and Spirit is not identical with the *testimonium*, but the *testimonium* is one of the facets of the doctrine of the Word and Spirit. This doctrine sets forth the fundamental relationship of the Holy Spirit to the Word of God (oral, tradition, or written).

Although Luther's and Calvin's followers disagreed over the details of this doctrine, they agreed to the doctrine as such. The Word and Spirit was the frontal attack of Protestantism against Romanism and the papacy. Both from a study of the Scripture and from the outcome of Roman-Protestant polemics, the Reformers were driven to postulate the doctrine and to develop it.

The union (German *Zusammengehörigkeit*, "belonging-togetherness") of Word and Spirit is itself rooted in the biblical doctrine of revelation. Revelation is given in two actions: the objective truth as such, and an inward rev-

---

1 Cf. Gordon Rupp, "Word and Spirit," *Archiv für Reformationsgeschichte*, XLIX (1958), 13-25.

elation enabling the human mind to grasp revelation as revelation. The objective revelation becomes appropriated by means of an inward revelation. This demands the closest relationship between objective and subjective revelation, which takes concrete form in the doctrine of Word and Spirit. The Word has temporal priority, for it is the necessary condition for the work of the Spirit. (The debate about special cases wherein the Spirit may work without the Word is not within our scope.) This Word has been brought into existence by the Holy Spirit (II Pet. 1:21, *pheromenoi* — moved, driven by the wind rather than in the sense of carried). The Spirit then *repeats* his own word in the human heart by the process of illumination. Narrowly conceived, this is the *testimonium*. Broadly conceived, it is the continuous use of the Scriptures by the Spirit in all of his operations.

The Scriptures were defended by the Reformers as *autopistic*, i.e., the Bible was Scripture in its own right. This was stated in opposition to Romanism, which claimed that the individual could not know that the Scriptures were the Word of God unless he were informed by the infallible Church. To the contrary, the Scriptures are the Word of God by virtue of their inspiration, and this inspired character was so intrinsic to them that they did not need the approval of the Church. *The resident autopistia of Scripture makes it suitable to be the instrument of the Spirit.* It is at this point that historic orthodoxy finds a serious fault with the neo-orthodox version of the *testimonium,* for the latter doctrine of Scriptural inspiration does not render Scripture suitable for use as the instrument of the Spirit.

But Calvin and Reformed orthodoxy (when not affected by rationalistic orthodoxy) have always insisted upon the *instrumental* character of Scripture. The Bible is a set of symbols. As a literary document it may persuade only as other literature may persuade. It may greatly influence the reader or it may leave him cold and unaffected. The power of any book to persuade is based upon many factors (e.g., style, cogency, thoroughness, moving illustrations) but they are all finally human. In itself the Bible is a record, a book, a document. It possesses no magical powers to influence the human mind.

It does not flash signals from heaven into the human soul. Without the Spirit it is a dead letter (so Calvin and Luther emphatically taught). But when the Spirit uses the Scripture as its instrument (based on the union of Word and Spirit), then the Word is efficacious. There can be no mechanical explanation of Scripture, as if the Scriptures contained a magical or mystical power for affecting the human mind. The Spirit is indispensable for the efficacious working of the Word.

By the same token of the union of Word and Spirit, the Spirit is mute without the Word. He can only make groanings which cannot be framed into speech. The Scriptures are indispensable for the working of the Spirit. To isolate Scripture from the Spirit, or the Spirit from Scripture, is theologically mischievous. Even those verses which speak of the power of the Word of God (Isa. 55, Heb. 4) must not be interpreted apart from the doctrine of the union of Word and Spirit. The true knowledge of God is gained with a teacher and a grammar, the Holy Spirit and the Sacred Writings.

This notion of Word and Spirit (with the emphasis on the instrumental character of Scripture) is contrary to Romanism, which so combines Church and Spirit as to either tragically weaken the union of Word and Spirit or utterly destroy it. The divinity of the Roman Church is entrusted to philosophical proofs in the "preamble of faith" and hence to a rationalistic procedure. Catholicism cannot really find place for a strong doctrine of Word and Spirit without destroying her doctrine of the union of Spirit and Church. This notion is also contrary to both Lutheranism and Reformed orthodoxy whenever they attribute to Scripture a sacramental, magical, or mystical power, failing to assign all ministries of the Word of God to the Holy Spirit. The union of Word and Spirit is not substantial but instrumental.[2] This notion

2 The Reformed theologians protested against the sacramental power which some Lutheran theologians attributed to Scripture. Kuyper, writing with reference to this, said: "By itself the Bible is nothing but a carrier and a vehicle, or, if you please, the instrument prepared by God, by which to attain His spiritual purpose, but always through the ever-present working of the Holy Spirit" (*Principles of Sacred Theology*, p. 398).

is contrary to *any* sort of theological rationalism (be it any form of historic orthodoxy, or contemporary fundamentalism) which attributes an independent power to the words of Scripture separate from the Holy Spirit. The Word is an instrument, a collection of signs, and it is efficacious only as God gives it life, power, and light. Only God is Spirit, only God is person, and therefore only God can persuade within the heart.

Section 11 : *The* testimonium *and the authority of Scripture*

From the perspective of history the most important aspect of the *testimonium* is its displacement of the Roman Catholic Church as the cause of our Christian certainty in the gospel and Scripture and its replacement by the Holy Spirit. Calvin first put the Scriptures *over* the Church; made the government of the Church by the Word as the sign of the true Church; invested the Scripture with *autopistia* and *aksiopiston;* and located the certainty of the Christian in the *testimonium* and not in the utterance of the Roman Catholic Church. We must now pursue this further and see how the *testimonium* relates itself to the total Scripture as it becomes authoritative to the Christian.

When revelation is received, its contents are not only known and believed, but there is always the tacit assumption that what is known and what is believed is the truth of God. When a man possesses revelation subjectively realized, he possesses it with full assurance of its truthfulness (*plērophoria,* plenitude of conviction that something is true). The experiences of Noah and Abraham can be understood only with the further understanding that with the revelations granted them was also granted a *plērophoria* as to their contents.

In the inward reception of revelation this *plērophoria* is always presumed. Revelation received *as revelation* is received as truth, the truth of God. Illumination is a capacity granted to us that we may see something as truth which we may have heard a hundred times before. Revelation, illumination, and truth are one piece. We cannot think of revelation as untrue, nor of illumination as illuminating a falsehood. Revelation and illumination directly imply the veracity of the contents of the revelation.

The *testimonium* makes precise the structure of revelation as illumination, as the perception of truth, as the realization óf the veracity of the contents of revelation. Certainly the truth as such must exist prior to illumination, and conversely, the truth is not grasped as such without the event of illumination. And the ready manner in which the New Testament *identifies* truth with the divine revelation and the gospel is not to be underestimated (e.g., II Cor. 6:7, Eph. 1:13, Col. 1:5, II Tim. 2:15, James 1:18).

The sinful human mind cannot find the truth of God in nature nor the Word of God in Scripture. It can speak only out of its own sin-marred contents, and this dare not be equated with the divine veracity. In fact, the human mind in sin cannot differentiate between human error and the Word of God, for it treats Scripture as just another book, and its contents as the mere opinions of Jews and Christians — or at best as elevated religious literature. Therefore there must be a medicine which overcomes this malady; there must be a power which leads the sinful mind from error to truth; and the divine remedy and the divine power is the *testimonium*.

The *testimonium* may occur wherever God's truth exists. It is not bound to truth in written form. Prior to Moses men enjoyed the *testimonium* as they did on the day of Pentecost. But once the truth is cast into written form (by the Spirit!), then the Spirit of God works with the written Word. The truth of God may come to us in song, in sermon, in sacrament, or in testimony, but when the revelation is inscripturated, all such media must be referable back to Scripture. Calvin and Luther both had a high regard for the preached word of God and considered it as a means of grace (*Gnadenmittel*), but every such sermon must have its content traceable back to Sacred Writ.

To sum up at this point: if the Spirit witnesses in truth, if he grants the illumination which accompanies revelation, then when that truth and that revelation become written, the Spirit works with the written Word. Our investigation of the scriptural references concerning the witness of the Spirit revealed that this was no narrow doctrine, but a very complex one. However, it is a tightly-knit complex. Perhaps it is best to call it one truth with many facets. The *testimonium* must be grasped as a *unity in complexity*, and *a complexity in unity*.

(i) When the precise, personal content of the *testimonium* is specified, *it is Jesus Christ;* for he is Lord, the Son of God, God manifest in the flesh.

(ii) When we consider the theological content (*Gotteslehre*) of the witness it is a *knowledge of God* (Matt. 11:27, II Cor. 4:4), although of a christological character (i.e., the God and Father of our Lord Jesus Christ).

(iii) When we reflect upon the consciousness of the person in whom the witness is taking place, it is the cry, "Father." Here is the *testimonium* in its intensely personal and soteriological character. He who cries "Father" (Gal. 4:6) also cries "Jesus is Lord" (I Cor. 12:3).

(iv) When we consider the content of the witness as revelation, the content is the *truth*, or the *word*, or the *gospel*, or the *mystery of God*, or the *testimony of God*, or the *truth of the gospel*, or as in I Corinthians 2:1ff., *revelation as such*, or as in I John 5:6, *the public life of Christ*.

(v) When we consider the *testimonium* from the standpoint of the purposes of God, its content is the *New Covenant* (II Cor. 3).

These are not five witnesses but one witness. Just as John says the witness of the water and the blood and the Spirit are one witness (I John 5:6ff.), so these five are one witness. And *any one of them may represent the whole*. He who says Jesus is Lord also says that he has seen the Father; and he who has seen the Father acknowledges that in Christ are hid all the mysteries of the Godhead. And he who knows the Father through the Son and the Son through the Father has entered into life and has also been united to God in the New Covenant. It is the seamless robe of the *testimonium* where each strand runs into every other strand.

The crucial matter at this point is that the truth of the Gospel has been put into written form. And, furthermore, the New Covenant has been put into written form

(cf. Matt. 26:28, I Cor. 11:23-34, and Heb. 8:6-13).
Furthermore again: the apostles have intentionally put
their witness into writing (Luke 1:1-4, and John 20:31.
The very existence of the Gospels is further proof).

Therefore, *the Sacred Scriptures are taken intimately
into the very bosom of the testimonium so that he who
says, "Abba, Father," will eventually say, "this Book is
God's truth." He who has the part shortly possesses the
whole.*

Our salvation may come to us in a number of ways: it
may come by a quiet reading of Scripture; by the customary preaching of the minister; by the impetus of an
evangelistic service; by the personal word of a Christian;
or by an accident of life which throws us unexpectedly
into the hearing of the gospel. When we believe, the
truth of the gospel is sealed in our hearts by the Holy
Spirit. We not only believe but we have a conviction in
our hearts that we have believed the truth. The certainty
of our personal salvation, and the certainty of the truthfulness of the gospel message which brought us our salvation, are one! Our divine Lord has given us a divine
salvation by the instrument of a divine message and by
the efficacious administration of the divine Spirit. The
entire set of concepts is permeated with the veracity
inherent in deity.

But when we seek to discover the source of this message,
we invariably find our way to Sacred Scripture. The
sermon, the song, the tract, the personal witness, the
Christian sacrament, all have their root in Sacred Scripture. We are led and driven to the conclusion that the
source of the message which saved our souls is higher than
the medium which brought us the message. We are thus
driven beyond minister, sermon, and sacrament to Holy
Scripture as the ground (not the cause, which is the Holy
Spirit) of our certainty, as the truth of God, and as the
authority for our faith and of our faith. In such a manner the *testimonium* becomes anchored in Sacred Scripture, and that is why faith in Jesus Christ is so vitally
and indestructibly linked to faith in Sacred Scripture. If
it is God who has saved our souls by the preaching of
the gospel, it is God who is the author of that Word which
contains the gospel. Thus the Spirit in bearing witness

that we are the sons of God inevitably leads to his witness of the divinity of Scripture.

The *testimonium*, which is related immediately to the gospel, relates itself immediately to the entire Scripture. According to some scholars the *testimonium* is a *direct* witness to the divinity of the Scripture, to the Bible as a bloc, a whole, an entity. But this is too violent a separation of the *testimonium* from its anchorage in christology and soteriology. The extension of the *testimonium* to the entire canon is a matter of logical action. We discover that revelation is one piece, so that if we take part, we are pledged to take all. If the *testimonium* centers in the gospel, we shortly see that it involves the Gospels, and then the entire New Testament, and then the Old Testament, for the New is continuous with the Old (Heb. 1:1-2). Or if we investigate such notions as revelation, or inspiration, or canonicity, we are also led to see that the *testimonium* in principle involves the total Scripture. Only when we have reached this point by logical action can we speak of the Scripture as a bloc or an entity.[3]

The *testimonium* is a direct part of the Protestant doctrine of authority. Broadly, the Protestant doctrine is the doctrine of Word and Spirit; narrowly conceived, it is the *testimonium*. The Scriptures represent the formal principle of authority; and the *testimonium* is the material principle. The principle of Chillingworth, "The Bible, I say, the Bible only, is the religion of Protestants"[4] is defective because it states only the formal principle of Protestantism and thus usually leads either to unwise biblicism or to theological rationalism or to bibliolatry — all three of which represent in their own way a displacement of the Holy Spirit. The classical Protestant doctrine of authority has been beautifully stated by one of the old dogmaticians, Voetius (1648-1669): "As there is no objective certainty about the authority of Scripture, save as infused and imbued by God the Author of Scripture, so we have no subjective certainty of it, no formal concept of the authority of Scripture, except from God

3 The issue raised here will be discussed later under the title, "Are There Two Witnesses?"

4 *The Religion of Protestants*, p. 463.

illuminating and convincing inwardly through the Holy Spirit. As Scripture itself, as if radiating an outward principle by its own light (no outsider intervening as principle or means of proof or conviction), is something *aksiopiston* [worthy of belief] or credible *per se* and *in se* — so the Holy Spirit is the inward, supreme, first, independent principle, actually opening and illuminating the eyes of the mind, effectually convincing us of the credible authority of Scripture from it, along with it, and through it, so that being drawn we run, and being passively convinced within, we acquiesce."[5]

Section 12: *The* testimonium *and the authority of God*

Faith never emerges spontaneously; it is always called into existence by something. Faith may be prompted into being by evidences, or by the persuasion of a friend, or by some emotional impulse, or by an intuition which comes from somewhere in our being. Faith is an inward motion toward some claim to truth, or factuality, or existence. We are not here concerned with the psychological or spiritual quality of faith, but with that which calls faith forth, with that which prompts faith into existence.

We wish to know why a person has directed his faith toward some particular claim. On the spiritual side faith may be very strong and courageous, but it may be at the same time incredibly irresponsible. The faith which throws itself entirely and devotedly into some cult without any investigation of the claims of the cult is a very irresponsible faith. To be free from the charges of obscurantism or fanaticism or credulity, a faith must give an acceptable accounting of itself. Unbelief may set no *a priori* limits on this accounting, but when faith gives its justification, it must be a responsible accounting.

What is the accounting for our faith in Christ, in the Christian gospel, in the Sacred Scriptures? It is of the very essence of the Christian faith to assert that the

5 H. Heppe, *Reformed Dogmatics*, pp. 25-26. Or, as Théo Preiss has said, the Spirit "makes the Bible a personal letter." "The Inner Witness of the Holy Spirit," *Interpretation*, VII (1953), 274. The relationship of the *testimonium* to the Protestant doctrine of authority was developed in my earlier book, *The Pattern of Religious Authority* (1957).

authority of the act of faith is God himself. God is our justification! It is axiomatic within Christianity that only God may speak for God! The seriousness of the issue, no less than our eternal destiny, demands something equal to the issue. We can demand no less than that there be a divine persuasion about the veracity of divine things. With Calvin we must feel as if God himself were reciting the truth to us (I,vii,1), or with Kuyper when he wrote: "What God Himself does not bear witness to in your soul personally . . . can never be known and confessed by you as divine."[6]

We believe that God persuades us of divine truth, and that therefore on both the outside and the inside, objectively and subjectively, we are dealing with divinity. This does not mean that God avoids earthly instruments, but rather that he enters them from the inside (mysteriously) and by them persuades us. This persuasion is not mystical nor magical nor theological legerdemain; but in our hearts the earthly medium receives such a divine reinforcement that the faith which is engendered is faith upon divine authority.

Concretely, what we have here is the *testimonium*. We have been efficaciously persuaded by the divine Spirit about the divine truth in a divinely inspired book. On the objective side, on the subjective side, on the part of the book, we are confronted with the divine. Therefore we may say that faith is prompted by a divine Spirit and is directed toward a divine truth. It is faith *in* the authority of God, and *on* the authority of God.

Nor must we fail to note that faith is made for Scripture and Scripture for faith. When God gave Scripture, he gave it so that it would be a fit object for faith (i.e., *autopistic*). And when he prompts faith, he prompts it in such a way that the believer becomes hungry for Scripture. He wants to live by every word which proceeds from the mouth of God (Matt. 4:4). He desires the "pure spiritual milk" (*to logikon adolon gala*, I Peter 2:2) of Sacred Scripture and as he matures he is ready for "solid food" (*stereas trophē*, Heb. 5:12). For with

6 *Principles of Sacred Theology*, p. 366. This is no apologetic for faith but a tracing of its genealogy.

David "his delight is in the law of the Lord, and on his law he meditates day and night" (Ps. 1:2).

Section 13: *The* testimonium *as a witness*

In an essay unique in the literature of the Holy Spirit Théo Preiss calls attention to the juridical terminology behind so much New Testament vocabulary about the Holy Spirit. "The fact has been singularly neglected, as much in exegesis as in dogmatics," he writes, "that almost all the terminology which is used to speak of the Spirit is in origin and in flavor more juridical than mystical or intellectual. The Spirit is before all things a *witness.*"[7] Mentioning the Spirit as the *other Paraclete,* Preiss says we are in "solid juridical terminology,"[8] and C. H. Dodd agrees when he says that the word "paraclete" is "properly a forensic term."[9] The verb, *parakalein,* shares in this legal derivation. J. H. Bernard shows how "paraclete" in general usage, and in New Testament usage, means three things: a *witness* (John 15:26), an *advisor* (John 16:8); and an *advocate* (John 16:13), and that it was not unusual among the Greeks for a man to make an appeal to God to be his paraclete.[10] And examination of the verb "convict" in John 16:8-11 again shows a strong legal coloring in the background.[11] This does not mean that in every instance these words have a strong juridical meaning, but that their background is juridical. Although the language usage moves away from the strict juridical meaning, the juridical association remains as a significant overtone.

It was Calvin, who saw clearly the role of the Holy Spirit as the witness *par excellence,* and taught that the Holy Spirit was the author of all witnessing. He makes the prophets and apostles witnesses and through them

7 "The Inner Witness of the Holy Spirit," *Interpretation,* VII (1953), 267. Italics are his.

8 *Ibid.,* p. 270.

9 *The Fourth Gospel,* p. 414.

10 "John" in *The International Critical Commentary,* II, 497.

11 Cf. Bernard, *ibid.,* II, 506; E. C. Hoskyns, *The Fourth Gospel,* p. 484; and Büchsel, *elegcho, Theologisches Wörterbuch zum Neuen Testament,* II, 470-437; Behm, *paraklētos, Theologisches Wörterbuch,* V, 798, 812.

creates the witness of the written Word. The Spirit gives men special gifts (prophecy and preaching) within the community of revelation to give further and special witness. The Spirit may then use these witnesses to convince other people of the truth of these contents.[12] However, in order to understand in what sense the work of the Spirit is a witness, we must recall the history of the word. Its first meaning is that of a witness giving evidence in court to settle a matter of fact. But a second meaning was noted by Aristotle, namely, to indicate the conviction of the witness and his intention to persuade others of the truth of his conviction. It is in this second sense that the Spirit is a witness. A remarkable verse at this point is I John 5:7, "And the Spirit is *the* witness, because the Spirit is *the* truth." The italics here emphasize the retention of the article in the Greek original. Paraphrasing we might render the verse as follows: "The efficacious Persuader is the Holy Spirit, because the Holy Spirit is absolutely veracious [and therefore can be absolutely trusted]."

The persuasion of the Spirit presumes the witness of the water and the blood (I John 5:6), i.e., the truth which already exists. This persuasion imparts nothing new, but rather testifies to that which is already the case.

Persuasion is the attempt of one person to influence another person by the use of various means — reasonings, evidence, illustrations; or various appeals to emotions, honor, family ties, love of country, etc. It is an attempt of one person to persuade another person to adopt his opinions, attitudes, or plan of action. The persuader is either convinced that he has the truth, or at least pretends that he has. *Truth* is the critical issue in witnessing, and that is why the apostle makes it emphatic that *the Spirit is truth* (I John 5:7).

How the Holy Spirit persuades and illuminates (for he does both) is a mystery. Our Lord taught as much (John 3:8). How one spirit affects another spirit is completely beyond us; we know nothing concretely or empirically about such an act. But the human spirit is open

12 Cf. Krusche, *Das Wirken des Heiligen Geistes nach Calvin*, p. 160.

to the divine Spirit with a directness more intimate than
anything we can imagine. Certainly it is a work below
the level of consciousness; and furthermore, it is an
intensely spiritual act upon the very center of man's
being. It is the work of the divine Spirit who touches
man at his deepest. This touching has to do with the
most serious matter of human existence: man's saving
relationship to God through Jesus Christ.

What is known to man is the *result* of the divine persuasion. This action is called many things in Scripture,
such as illumination, opening the eyes of the understanding, having the mind of Christ, etc. The result of this
action is a full conviction of the truth (*plērophoria*). And
this truth is very concrete: that Jesus Christ is the Son
of God (I John 5:20), that Jesus is Lord (I Cor. 12:3),
that the New Covenant is the truth of God (II Cor. 3),
or that I am God's child and he is my Father (Gal. 4:6).
This persuasion is not created by reason although it
touches my reason; it is not rooted in my senses although
the gospel is heard or read by the senses; nor is it directly
an emotional stirring, although we may be deeply stirred
when we cry, Abba, Father! It is through and through
a divine matter. The divine Spirit employs a divine
Word characterized as possessing divine perfections to
bring our minds to a full conviction of these matters.

The Church must then resist all improper attempts to
induce faith in the gospel and the Scriptures. It must
oppose the mechanical approach to Scripture which believes that the Scriptures in themselves automatically,
and separately from the Spirit, may evoke faith; and it
will oppose rationalistic attempts to compel faith in the
Scriptures without the persuasion of him who is *the* Witness, and *the* Truth (I John 5:7).

To be sure, the intensity of this persuasion differs from
Christian to Christian. There are those who add their
native dogmatism to the witness of the Spirit and appear
as hopelessly opinionated people. Others have a very
quiet and unobtrusive faith; and still others are like the
father of the epileptic who cried, "I believe; help my unbelief" (Mark 9:24). There is no teaching in the New
Testament that this witness is uniform in its psychologi-

cal effects. What *is* uniform teaching is that any and all saving conviction about the truthfulness of the Christian faith arises from the persuading work of the great Witness, the Spirit of truth.

Section 14: *The* testimonium *is internal*

The witness of the Spirit is called internal, or secret, or inner. This is where the New Testament locates it. In Galatians 4:6 it occurs in the heart (*kardia*); in Romans 8:16, in the spirit (*pneuma*); in I John 5:20, in the understanding (*dianoia*); and in I John 5:10, in ourselves (*en autō*).

The *testimonium* is, then, private. It cannot be shared, communicated, or objectified. The entire structure of the *testimonium* is revealed not in experience, but in the revelation. Therefore the Christian cannot simply deduce the *testimonium* from his own experience. The Christian can give an indirect witness to the *testimonium* by a recitation of his own conversion experience. Paul does not hesitate to give his own witness in describing his conversion experience (e.g., Acts 22 and 26). In the writing of his epistles he recited some important aspects of his experience of the grace of God in Jesus Christ (e.g., Gal. 1 and 2, or Phil. 3:1ff.). And it must also be emphasized that the Paul who wrote Rom. 8:15-16 and Gal. 4:6 had himself, out of his own experience, cried, "Abba, Father." Also John, who said that every Christian had an anointing within himself and had the witness within himself, had in himself the experiential counterparts of these divine actions. Although the witness of the Spirit is not capable of objectification (and is not intersubjective), nevertheless Christians can recite their own personal experiences which become indirect witnesses of the *testimonium*.

It is possible that one is aware of the very passage of Scripture which was the instrument of his illumination. Like Augustine he may be able to put his finger on a specific passage, such as Romans 13:14. Others may read this verse and not experience any movement of the Spirit, but by the very nature of the *testimonium* this does not tell against his own experience. Countless Christians may

point to specific verses or passages and date their deci-
sions of faith from the very moment they read the same
and encountered the grace of God in Jesus Christ. And
in giving testimony to this experience they again witness
indirectly to the *testimonium*.

There is no uniform procedure by which the Spirit bears
his witness. We presume that it is as varied and individual as human beings themselves are. There are Christians raised in a Christian home who have never experi-
enced a transition from unbelief to belief. There are
others whose faith has come in so many small steps that
they cannot tell which step crossed the invisible line from
unbelief into saving faith. But the import of the *testimonium* is the same in each case. The psychological and
historical antecedents are not the *testimonium* itself, and
such variations are insignificant.

The important thing is to note that the *testimonium* is
by its very nature a divine and *secret* work and therefore
incapable of objectification. It is an easy temptation to
brand the *testimonium* as subjective, but from the theological side the privacy of the *testimonium* is its very
strength, for it is by the same token *immediate* and therefore *certain* and *sure*. Preiss has stated this so excellently: "Between God and man there is no intermediary;
God does not send to the earth a being detached from
himself; he does not give something to man; he gives
himself, with all his great Fatherly heart, in the Son.
And then the Father and the Son give themselves entirely
to man in the Spirit. Thus the distance between God
and man is at one and the same time safeguarded and
conquered, and a communion is established which has
nothing to do with an identity of pantheistic substance,
a communion at the same time most reserved and most
profound between person and person."[13]

Section 15: *The* testimonium *and Pentecost*

Jesus promised that when he returned to the Father,
he would send another Counselor, the word "another"

---

13 *Op. cit.*, p. 265.

indicating that he himself was the first Counselor.[14] The Holy Spirit would be to all the disciples what Christ had been to the twelve (John 14:16). The Spirit came on Pentecost, and as we read the account of his coming, we discover two different sorts of statements about the Spirit: phenomenal and theological.

The Spirit did not come quietly or secretly. Rather, he broke out of his hiddenness to manifest himself as a palpable phenomenon. Not he, of course, but his signs were manifest; nevertheless they were signs of him. The sound of a mighty wind commenced in heaven to indicate the point of its origin, and it filled the house to show the point of its termination — from *heaven* to a *house!* Not unlike the mystery of Christmas — from *heaven* to a *stable!* This sound appealed to the ear. Next appeared the tongues of fire which appealed to the eye. He came not only in power, in the wind; but he came with a message, in the tongue of fire. And this was followed by the bestowing of the gift of tongues — an appeal to the mind. Whether the miracle took place in the tongues of the disciples or in the ears of the listeners (Kuyper) is not the present issue.

There was a happy intersection of phenomena, appealing to the ear, the eye, and the mind which reduced to a vanishing minimum the possibility of deception. Further, the manifestation was not given to only one person. The sound filled the *house!* The fiery tongue was given to *each!* They *all* spoke in tongues! And they spilled out into the street in their enthusiasm and ecstasy, making it a matter of *public manifestation!* "And at this sound the multitude came together" — Parthians, Medes, Elamites, Mesopotamians, Judeans, Cappadocians, Phrygians, Pamphylians, Egyptians, Libyans, Cyrenians, Romans, Cretans, and Arabians (Acts 2:5-11). Nor did these signs

14 The word *paraklētos* is discussed by Behm (*op. cit.*) at some length. It is used only by John, of Jesus and the Holy Spirit. Historically it has meant a lawyer (*Anwalt*), a helper (*Beistand*), and an intercessor or advocate (*Fürsprecher*). Because of its long and involved history, the word has become difficult to translate, complains Behm. Most German translators avoid the transliteration, *Paraklete*, and prefer *Beistand* or *Helfer*. But, Behm warns, the notion of *Fürsprecher* hovers over any other word used to translate *paraklētos* as the fundamental meaning of the word (p. 812).

stop at the day of Pentecost, for we hear of some of them being repeated (Acts 4:31, 10:44-48, 19:6). This signifies that the Spirit really came, for the repetition of the signs signifies the abiding presence of the Holy Spirit. He is here as a permanent gift to the Church, a resident of the world until the Savior returns.

But the phenomenal aspects of the day of Pentecost are no less important than the *theological* assertions made by Peter. These are christological assertions, for Peter says much about Jesus Christ; they are trinitarian assertions, for Peter speaks of the Father, the Son, and the Spirit; they are soteriological assertions, for Peter speaks about sin and salvation; and they are pneumatological assertions, for Peter discusses the coming and the giving of the Holy Spirit.

It is, first, a *coming* of the Spirit of God. This is no ordinary event, nor an extraordinary event, but an absolutely *cardinal* event. It is one of the few great events in the total scope of redemption. It is like creation, and the fall, and the call of Abraham, and the exodus, and the incarnation, and the cross, and the resurrection, and the return of Christ. This is the gift of the Father to the Son who in turn gives to the disciples (Acts 2:33). Therefore, the Spirit is poured out to emphasize a real, a great, a historical coming of God's Spirit.

Second, it is the coming of the Spirit for *all believing flesh*. The ancient and necessary distinctions and divisions of the old dispensation are now obliterated by the outpouring of the Spirit of Christ. Acts 2 specifies that sons, daughters, young men, old men, menservants, and maidservants shall receive the Spirit. This is spiritually and theologically consanguine with Paul's remarks in Galatians 3:27-28 that there are no human distinctions in Jesus Christ. There are no Jews, Greeks, slaves, freemen, males, or females, but all are one in Christ. This can only mean, from the perspective of Pentecost, that Jews, Greeks, slaves, freemen, men, and women all receive the Holy Spirit. In the Christian faith the total Christian community severally receives the Holy Spirit. We are "a chosen race, a royal priesthood, and a holy nation" (I Pet. 2:9) to our God.

Third, the Spirit is promised to all who believe the

gospel (Acts 2:38). The Spirit is not a special gift for one generation, nor one land, nor one race. He is offered as the promise of the Father, the gift of God, to all men wherever and whenever they live, and always in terms of the gospel of Jesus Christ.

The *testimonium* is therefore grounded in Pentecost. The individual experience of the Holy Spirit must be set in the total perspective of Pentecost. "Hence the outpouring of the Holy Spirit is the crowning event of all the great events of salvation," penned Kuyper, "because it reveals *subjectively,* i.e., in individual persons, the grace revealed hitherto objectively."[15] At Pentecost the mighty Wind of heaven came into the world. He is here, in the world, as the personal and spiritual Power of God. He moves invisibly, as hidden as the wind, but nonetheless here as the Helper, the Counselor, the Breath of God. And being here, he bears his sacred witness. Pentecost is the day of his coming. He entered the world with remarkable and indubitable signs. And being here, he steps quietly, secretly, mysteriously into our own hearts by the *testimonium.*

Section 16: *The* testimonium *and the Church*

One of the most remarkable features of the history of the Church and the history of theology is that the theologian (John Calvin) who developed so clearly the doctrine of the *testimonium,* which he opposed to the *magisterium* of the Church, nevertheless is one of the greatest churchmen the Church has ever produced. If one reads Calvin and Luther and then reads Catholic polemics against them, one can only judge that in far too many instances Catholic scholarship is convulsed by an irrational antipathy to these two names. How contradictory are the charges of "subjectivism" or "individualism" or "religious anarchy" made by Catholic scholars to Calvin's great doctrine of the Church and his careful refutation of "subjectivism," "individualism," and "religious anarchy." The author of the *testimonium* has one of the strongest doctrines of the Holy Spirit and the Church to

15 *The Work of the Holy Spirit,* p. 208. Italics are his.

be found in the history of theology.[16]   As Krusche points
out, Calvin believed in the togetherness (*zusammengehören*)
of Spirit, Word, and Church and therefore strongly opposed religious individualism in two forms: (i) the enthusiasts who were concerned with the Spirit separate
from the Word, and (ii) those who wanted all their religion from personal Bible study.   Every Christian needs
to hear the Word *in the preaching ministry of the
Church.*[17]   And speaking to the same point Pannier wrote:
"To eliminate completely the role of the Church in favor
of the Scriptures had not been done by any of the Protestant doctors, and the very idea of this substitution was
foreign — not to say contrary — to the principle of the
Reformers."[18]   It was standard Reformed doctrine that
the Spirit was not only the Spirit of the Word of God,
but also of the Church of God.

The New Testament teaches very clearly that the Holy
Spirit is given to every Christian, for if a man does not
have the Holy Spirit, he does not belong to Christ (Rom.
8:9).   And it is just as clear that the Holy Spirit is the
Spirit of the body of Christ, the Church of Christ.   We
have been baptized together into one body by one Spirit,
and we have all been made to drink of one Spirit (I Cor.
12:13).   The members of the one body of Christ are
asked to "maintain the unity of the Spirit in the bond of
peace" (Eph. 4:2).   The temple of God composed of many
living stones is inhabited by the Holy Spirit (Eph. 2:22).
Therefore those verses which speak of each Christian as a
bearer of the Spirit must be matched by those which
speak of the Spirit as the unseen but real unity of all believers.   The Spirit forms us into a temple, a spiritual
community, a body dwelling in each of us individually
and corporately.

The *testimonium* is not to be isolated from the Church.
This *testimonium* is given within the Church, for it is
the possession of *all* believers.   It is not the possession
of the spiritually alert, but the common heritage of all.

16 Cf. Krusche's nicely written and carefully documented discussion under "Der Heilige Geist und die Heilsgemeinde." *Op. cit.*,
pp. 300ff.

17 *Ibid.*, pp. 302-303.

18 *Op. cit.*, p. 19.

Revelation tells us, then, that the *testimonium* is the experience of each believer within the conditions of his own personality, his own age, his own sex, and his own historico-sociological background. From the divine perspective, however, the *testimonium* is the same for a believer in Derbe in the first century as it is for a believer in Tokyo in the twentieth; it is the same for a Hottentot as it is for a Park Avenue sophisticate.

The witness is given by the Spirit who forms the body of Christ. He is the common bond among believers. If we are living stones, he may be likened to living mortar which transforms individual bricks into a spiritual temple. The *testimonium* which is personal and private is yet the work of the Spirit in the common life of the Church. According to the pneumatological doctrine of the Church, the *testimonium* is personal to the core, but not individualistic; it is private, but utterly free from the spirit of religious anarchy; it occurs unseen in the heart, but drives the Christian into the fellowship of the visible, local church. It is subjective (as all things intensely personal, vital, spiritual, and meaningful are), but because the *testimonium* is the witness of the Holy Spirit of the Church, and because in a real sense it occurs within the Church, the *testimonium* does not lead to subjectivism.

Section 17: *The universality of the* testimonium

The prophecy of Joel cited in Peter's pentecostal sermon states that God will pour his Spirit out upon all flesh. This corresponds to the truth that God loves the world (John 3:16) and desires all men to be saved (I Tim. 2:4, *pantas anthrōpous*); and that the death of Christ was a propitiation for the sins of the whole world (I John 2:2, *hilasmos . . . peri holou tou kosmou*). The kingdom of God no longer limits its central attention to the Jewish people, nor does the worship of God confine itself to the temple at Jerusalem (John 4:21), nor do the purposes of God end at the boundaries of Palestine (Acts 1:8, "to the end of the earth," *eōs eschatou tēs gēs*). The universal character of the love of God and the death of Christ means the universal outpouring of the Holy Ghost and the international character of the Christian Church. The *testimonium* is as universal as the gospel, the Church, and the outpouring of the Holy Spirit.

But there is another character to the universality of the gospel. It is universal with respect to the individual differences among people. It does not respect sex, for male and female alike are offered the gospel; it does not respect age, for children and grandparents are counted among the believers; it does not respect social distinctions, for harlots, publicans, and noblemen press into the kingdom of God; and it does not put a premium on ignorance nor a penalty on learning, for both wise and foolish are called. Because of the insufferable character of human pride (cf. I Cor. 8:1, "knowledge puffs up"), there are more foolish called than the powerful and the noble (I Cor. 2:26ff.) ; and because the rich are so tempted to "set their hopes on uncertain riches" (I Tim. 6:17), more poor are called than rich (James 2:5). But the reception of the gospel and the *testimonium* are spiritual matters and therefore are universal in character. Every believer is a recipient of the *testimonium* within the characteristics of his own self and its historical and social conditions, but the *testimonium* is not conditioned upon any intellectual qualifications beyond those necessary for responsible human nature.

Christian certainty, the product of the *testimonium*, is the possession of all God's children. It may vary in intensity, but the basic reality of it is universal in character, and the increase of its intensity is not gained solely by a deeper intellectual grasp of the Christian faith. Great Christian conviction — sainthood and martyrdom — is to be found in all sorts of Christian persons.

What is discussed here is "the professor or the Christian" controversy. According to Roman Catholic theology a man is moved toward the Roman Catholic Church by the *Preamble of Faith*. By the right use of reason the unregenerate man can prove the existence of God and some of his attributes, the existence of the soul and its immortality, and the divine authority of the Roman Catholic Church. But Roman Catholic scholars are always ready to admit (as Aquinas himself did) that ordinary people are not capable either of constructing such a proof or following that of the scholar. Certainty is thus restricted to professors, so to speak. Although Roman Catholic theologians attempt to cover up for the layman, so that he has virtually the same assurance as the professor, they are not convincing. On their premises only the professor who can follow learned philosophical arguments can really enjoy certainty with no alloy.

Such a doctrine of certainty runs counter to the entire structure of the *testimonium*, and the objection to it applies not only to Romanism but to all Protestant systems which would confine certainty to professors. The great Reformed theologians, such as Kuyper, Warfield, Lecerf, and C. W. Hodge, have asserted that Christian certainty cannot be the sole possession of professors. Scholarship *per se* cannot be the basis for our certainty of the gospel, for the gospel and the *testimonium* do not make us professors but Christians. It is not learning or scholarship which enables a man to find the Word of God in Scripture, but the *testimonium;* and the *testimonium* is given in terms of the gospel. ·On the contrary, learned investigations seldom lead to faith or to the dissipation of doubt; rather, they increase the possible places where the Christian faith may be equivocated.

Furthermore, the disguised intellectualism which attempts to limit real certainty to those who read the Hebrew and Greek must also be resisted. The gospel can be readily translated into other languages and so evoke saving faith, and therefore "the child of God feels *irresistibly* that in the matters which concern eternity, Greek and Hebrew cannot have the last word."[19] The only conclusion to be drawn is that just as the gospel is

19 Kuyper, *The Work of the Holy Spirit*, p. 192. Italics are his. Of course Kuyper had no intention at all of deprecating the study of Hebrew and Greek. He only objected when the use of the languages was by an "unbearable intellectual clericalism." And Calvin, the theologian of the *testimonium*, is no founder of a spiritual or theological intellectualism; and in his doctrine of the priority of knowledge in faith he is thereby no founder of intellectualism. Calvin felt that the will could not act, nor the emotions respond, until the will and the emotions had been enlightened by the intellect. However, it is Krusche's opinion that Calvin is closer to the voluntarists of the middle ages than to Aquinas, who taught the primacy of the intellect. *Op. cit.*, p. 263.

universal in every way, so is the *testimonium;* and every believer possesses the certainty of the *testimonium* because he is a Christian and not because he is a professor.

Section 18: *The* testimonium *as perception*

There is an irreducible intuitive element in all knowledge, though most philosophical schools would like to purge intuition from their theory of knowledge. Even logic is ineffectual, however, unless the pupil *sees* how the conclusions follow. Reading a sentence word for word, as a beginner does in a foreign language, does not yield the meaning of the sentence; the reader must *see* the words in their relationships to gather the sense of the sentence. Without the function of intuition in the knowledge process little would be learned. The *testimonium* has the character of intuition, and not that of discursive reasoning. It is a direct apprehension of something as true, and not a conclusion at the end of a short or long chain of reasoning.

Man's difficulty as sinner is not that he cannot properly calculate with logical symbols. His problem is not that he has lost a certain ability to reason. If this were the case, the divine remedy would be a course in logic. Man's real difficulty is that he is spiritually blind: the truth of God does not impress the sinful mind for what it is. Sinful man always equivocates the truth one way or another. The remedy does not consist in attempting to outwit his equivocations. The remedy consists in the restoration of spiritual vision and sight, of the opening of ears and eyes resulting in an intuition of the truth of God.

The *testimonium* is, then, no audible voice; no sudden exclamation that "the Bible is the word of God"; no miracle removing us out of our normal routine of creaturely existence; no sudden surge of a religious emotion; no revelation with flashing lights and new ideas; no religious experience as such; no creation of some new or special organ of spiritual vision; but rather, it is the touch of the Holy Spirit upon native and resident powers of the soul which had been rendered ineffectual through sin. It is an opening of the eyes resulting in an intuition of seeing; it is the unplugging of the ears resulting in an intuition of hearing. It is the removal of a veil; it is

light dissipating darkness. It is illumination granting
the powers of spiritual perception. The total inward man
now *sees* revelation as revelation; he *intuits* truth as truth;
he *hears* Scripture as the truth of God. The *testimonium*
acts with the simplicity (characteristic of an intuition)
of seeing or hearing; and results in the certainty of an
object clearly seen or a sound distinctly heard.

But this intuition is not a seeing of so many theological
sentences as such; it is primarily directed toward Jesus
Christ and his gospel. What is actually seen and heard
is first of all Jesus Christ, and we see him and his gospel
in a profoundly spiritual manner. We see him and his
truth *for* us, as *including* us, as *intending* us. In this intuition we are not being introspective, pondering over
what is taking place within us, but we are in a perceptive
and receptive mood.

The result of this intuition is *plērophoria* — spiritual
certainty. It is not solely a granting of spiritual vision,
for the persuasion of the Spirit is part of the *testimonium*.
It is at the same time an intuition and a persuasion.
What we have said of the juridical terms employed in
connection with the Holy Spirit must be here called to
mind. The result of this *plērophoria* is that the Christian
accepts the gospel as the final truth of God and rests content in it. He does not thirst again for other religious
waters. And because this *plērophoria* is not achieved by
sense or reason, it is not endangered by sense or reason.
It is the gift of the Holy Spirit and therefore rests in the
simplicity and certainty of a spiritual intuition.

Philosophers like to present the sensing of a colored
patch as the type of an indubitable experience. What is
more real than the deliveries of the healthy eye as it fastens
itself upon one simple object? Occasional illusions of
our vision do not detract from the certainty of sensing
this vivid colored patch! Thus we live every day in the
absolutized certainty of our sense perceptions. However, other philosophers find their point of indubitability
in some form of logic or discursive reasoning. If everything is in logical order, then the conclusions necessarily
follow (or in empirical matters, follow with a high order
of probability).

But the *testimonium* is not a sensation, nor the distillation of sensations in the form of abstractions; nor is it the product of a logical calculation; nor is it the product of the application of logic to historical or sensorial materials. It is the product of an operation upon us by the Holy Spirit. It is the freeing of a faculty deranged by sin, and the result is a spiritual perception.

No one would deny that the Word of God enters consciousness by the senses (hearing or reading), and no one denies that the *testimonium* calls our rational powers into play. It is an action which affects the total man. It results in thinking differently, evaluating differently, feeling differently, and willing differently, but in the *testimonium* our minds, wills, and feelings function ministerially and not magisterially.

The result of the *testimonium* is a spiritual certainty which is stronger than sense or reason. It is stronger because it is the action of the Spirit of God upon us, and not merely our action. It is stronger because the Holy Spirit can act deeper in us and upon us that we can on ourselves, or than others can upon ourselves. It is stronger because it is the Holy Spirit doing something for us which we cannot do for ourselves. It is stronger because it is an opening of the eyes of the understanding; an unplugging of the ears of the soul; a removal of a veil from the mind; a persuasion by the divine barrister, the *Paraklētos*, the *Advocatus*, the *Fürsprecher*, *l'avocat*.

Therefore the *testimonium* is not capable of proof. For proof we would have to appeal to something sensory, but this is excluded by the nature of the *testimonium*. Or we would have to appeal to experience, but this would only reveal that different people have different religious experiences. The *testimonium* is autonomous within itself and therefore not capable of any sort of proof.

What the Christian theologian does is to set forth the structure of the *testimonium*. This structure is given within special revelation. He investigates the verses which discuss it. He may then proceed to the writings of theologians who have busied themselves with the *testimonium*. He has as relevant but not compelling data, the deliveries of his own experience of God's grace, and the reports of his fellow Christians. And when he is through, he attempts to set forth the structure of the *testimonium* as clearly and faithfully as he can. It is not a proof, for if it were a proof, it would be competing with the *testimonium;* it is rather a witness to the *testimonium.*

The intuition of the *testimonium* is at first directed toward the gospel, but it afterward opens up to the total range of the Christian revelation. It is not a flash that is soon over with, but it is an anointing which abides (I John 2:27). God's word and God's truth are in us as permanent residents. Therefore the Christian reads *all* of Sacred Scripture with illumined eyes. He is now concerned with "spiritual truths" (I Cor. 2:13), and as a spiritual man he can discern *all* things (v. 15). He now has the mind of Christ and can find Christ in all the Scriptures. When the veil is removed (II Cor. 3:12ff.), he may read the total corpus of Scripture with seeing and knowing eyes.

He thus has the spiritual power to perceive Scripture as the truth of God. Psalm 119 is devoted to this wonderful subject. The Christian *wants to live* by every word which has proceeded from the mouth of God (Matt. 4:4). Scripture has become to him pure spiritual milk (I Pet. 2:2), and upon spiritual maturation it is his strong food (Heb. 5:14). In the language of Calvin, just as the tongue can taste sweet and bitter, and the eye can see black and white, so the Christian can "taste" and "see" the truth of God in Scripture (I,vii,2).

Section 19: *The* testimonium *and ourselves*

The *testimonium* is something which happens within us. The objective reality of our justification in Jesus Christ, the impossibility of grounding salvation in any human merit, and the objectivity of the *testimonium* must not obscure the parallel truth that the *testimonium* happens in Christians and to Christians. God does not believe for us, though faith is a gift of God. God does not will for us, for what we will is our doing. "This faculty is not capable of compulsion," wrote Owen correctly, for "if it be compelled it is destroyed."[20] Believing and willing are peculiarly the actions of the human person. The

20 J. Owen, *The Holy Spirit,* p. 184.

testimonium is not a vicarious believing or a vicarious willing or a vicarious thinking.

The *testimonium* is something which concretely happens to Christians. It does really and truly happen to them. It makes a genuine difference in their consciousness. In Kierkegaard's language, it is *truth for me*. It could not be a witness unless it had this character. The *testimonium* is a movement from the divine Spirit upon our spirit. We are not able to dissect it out of our consciousness, for its origin and manner of working eludes us. But it leaves a real *depositum* in the being of the Christian. And this *depositum* is there in such a way that it belongs peculiarly to the Christian. It cannot exist as a textbook reality, but only as a real spiritual certainty.

The *testimonium* comes to us as persuasion, which is a form of influence directed toward free persons. It therefore respects the human person and does not force his will. Only those who are incapacitated in some manner (e.g., criminals, insane, children) can be compelled honorably. And only honorable modes of persuasion show respect for the full rights of the human person. Therefore whenever the *testimonium* occurs, it respects human freedom and dignity.

The *testimonium* happens to men in their concrete existence. It happens to Christians in such a manner that it makes a difference in their lives, but not in such a way that in turn the Christian can extract the structure of the *testimonium* out of his own consciousness or experience. When the *testimonium* enters the mind, it mixes with the contents which are already there. Whenever it happens to a man, it does not change him from who, where, and what he is. Only God sees the total workings of the *testimonium*. If we as Christians introspect ourselves, all we discover is more of ourselves. Only in Scripture is the *structure* of the *testimonium* given.

The content of the *testimonium* is the gospel of Jesus Christ. The content is not some extraordinary experience, nor some magical inbreaking upon our consciousness. Whenever there is a spiritual quickening of the mind, it always occurs by the instrumentality of the Word of God, and concretely, the gospel. It touches the total man and affects the entire range of his powers and faculties. It is no losing of one's individuality, nor the stultification nor the overpowering of any human faculty or power; it is rather the freeing, the releasing, the redeeming of those powers and faculties back toward their original created purity. It is not a complete restoration, but it is sufficient to allow the believing sinner to see the truth as truth. It must come in at least this measure to every Christian, but never in any fixed formula or inflexible psychological pattern (as revivalists and theologians are alike tempted to say). The concrete experiences of two Christians are never the same.

If the content of the gospel is Jesus Christ, the *intention* of the gospel is to bind the mind of the believer to the authority of the New Testament, and to the lordship of Jesus Christ. These are not two separate entities. The New Testament is the Word of our Lord, and therefore one of the signs of saving faith is a willingness to keep his teachings (I John 2:3-5) which are contained in the New Testament. That "Jesus is Lord" is not only the confession of a believing heart moved by the Spirit, but it is the standard of Christian obedience. The concrete desire to govern one's life by the teachings of Jesus Christ as preserved for us in the New Testament, and the concrete surrender to the Lordship of Jesus Christ, are witnessing marks of the *testimonium*.

The *testimonium* is related to the personal experiences of Christians. Although the structure and character of the *testimonium* are known only through Scripture, nevertheless the act of regeneration and the *testimonium* make a difference in the believer. But as indicated, these two occur *within* the total conditioning factors of each Christian, and their effects pour into Christian consciousness to mix with whatever else is there. The Christian, then, does not bear witness to the structure of the *testimonium;* he can only bear witness to his own personal experience. And this is not a reprehensible thing to do, for two reasons. First, giving our own personal experience of God's grace is one of the most effective ways of preaching the gospel. Second, it has apostolic example.

On two very important occasions Paul felt that his strongest move was to narrate the details of his conver-

sion: the first was when he addressed the mob on
the staircase in Jerusalem (Acts 22:1-21), and the second was when he had the important audience with
King Agrippa (Acts 26:1-29). We also find that Paul
felt free to cite his personal experience in his letters when
he thought it relevant. He defended his apostleship on
the basis that he had seen Jesus our Lord (I Cor. 9:1),
and had the boldness to list the appearance of Jesus to
him on the Damascus road as one of the official appearances of the risen Christ (I Cor. 15:8 — most scholars
take this list as the official list of appearances as accepted
by the Early Church). He summed up his conversion
tersely in Galatians 1:16 as God revealing his Son "in me."
When debating with the Judaizers, he felt called upon to
give some special details of his life before and after his
conversion (Phil. 3:1ff.), and in writing encouragement
to Timothy he narrated the sharp contrast between his
attitudes before conversion and after (I Tim. 1:11-15).

One's personal experience is the obverse side of the
work of the Holy Spirit. It represents the personal and
historically conditioned side of this divine work. Although not a datum from which we can extract the structure of the *testimonium* (which is found only in Scripture), it does represent the concrete reality of the
testimonium in human life. Thus our personal experience
of God's grace is a witness, not a compelling argument.
It, too, can be equivocated by psychologists and sociolo-
gists. Only the *testimonium* as it occurs in man's heart
is free from equivocation. In the experience of being
persuaded by the divine barrister, a man cannot doubt.

Section 20: *The* testimonium *and the indirection and
hiddenness of the Holy Spirit*

The great mystery of the Christian religion is God
manifest in the flesh, in the flesh of Jesus of Nazareth.
The Son of God is the manifesting one and the manifest
one. But the mystery of the Holy Spirit comes from the
fact that he is the power of God present and active, the
executive of the divine will, the Lord of all life, and the
immediate bearer and communicator of salvation, but
yet remains hidden. Here the Son and the Spirit stand
at antipodes. The Son is the one who manifested his

glory to the apostles (Matt. 17:2, John 2:11). The Spirit is like the wind, who moves invisibly (John 3:8).

Yet the Spirit has his signs. He is the dove at the baptism of the Savior, and in Acts 2 he comes with the signs of a rushing wind, a tongue of fire, and the gift of tongues. The writer to the Hebrews speaks of God bearing a witness to the message of the apostles by the gifts of the Holy Spirit (Heb. 2:4). But we have only a symbol — a dove; a sign — a mighty wind; and a gift — tongues, but never himself. He always wears the cloak of invisibility. These signs, however, have a real importance. The Spirit steps out of his hiddenness just enough to prevent us from reducing him to an abstraction, a powerless phantom. He is the "finger of God" (Luke 11:20, Matt. 12:28) — the concentrated, pointed power of Almighty God that can make a visible difference in the universe (Exod. 8:19), or eject Satan from his own kingdom.

He is the Wind of God. He is invisible, yet he is powerful. We can never know him manifestly, openly. Any proposed psychological or sociological studies of the workings or operations of the Holy Spirit are meaningless and preposterous. The reality investigated or tested will elude all such efforts to objectify it. The person who bears witness stands behind the veil of visibility. Any attempt to lift the curtain will achieve exactly nothing. Yet this hidden one is the power of God. His power is that fulness of omnipotence which is part of the divine majesty. Therefore, when thinking of the Holy Spirit, we must always keep together his *hiddenness* and *almightiness*.

Not only is the Spirit hidden, but his ministry is an indirect one. He will not speak of himself (*aph heautou*, John 16:13), i.e., he will not minister concerning himself, but "will glorify me" (v. 14). His operations terminate on Jesus Christ. This is the great humility of the Holy Spirit. "As a good witness [the Holy Spirit] will efface himself before the one of whom he testifies even as the Son effaces himself before his Father. I will say readily that the dominant trait of the Spirit is his perfect discreetness, his complete humility. And that is what explains the rather troublesome fact that we never visibly get the experience of the Holy Spirit himself, that he keeps before our eyes a silhouette so fleeting, a little vague and elusive."[21]

In this divine self-effacement the Spirit witnesses to Jesus Christ. His is a ministry of *indirection* in that it does not terminate on the Spirit but upon the Savior. Yet as a witness the Spirit comes with his credentials. To this extent there is a measure of *reflexive* witness about the Spirit in Scripture, so that we might understand his *directive* witness toward Jesus Christ. The Spirit who inspires Scripture must inspire certain passages about himself, that believers may know his actions and understand them. We must learn how and why we trust the witness of one who is so hidden and indirect.

We learn that he is the Spirit of truth, for he speaks as a perfectly veracious person (I John 5:7). He is the Spirit of God the Father, and the Spirit of Jesus Christ. Therefore he is in the Trinity and participates in all the attributes of deity. He is totally and completely one with the Father and the Son in being, reality, intentions, and purposes. Having such credentials of absolute veracity and unquestionable deity, he warrants our full and complete confidence.

The burden of the witness is God manifest in the flesh; the life, teachings, and death of the God-man; his atoning sacrifice and glorious resurrection; and his ascension and session at God's right hand. It is a witness about our justification, the forgiveness of our sins, our adoption into the divine family — all in and through Jesus Christ. Our consciousness is not of the Holy Spirit. He is at work in our hearts in his hiddenness and power, but he directs the eyes of our heart toward the Savior and toward the gift of salvation. We do not have a Spirit-consciousness; we have a Christ-consciousness. The *testimonium* does not ask the believer to look within to find the Spirit, but to look toward the Savior and his benefits. Only after the Spirit works do we discover his work, and this not through an inspection of our hearts. Because the *testimonium* is indirect and the Spirit's working is hidden, we know of his operations only by revelation. By means of the reflexive revelation the Spirit focuses temporarily

21 Preiss, *op. cit.*, p. 271.

upon himself so we may learn of the particular workings of the Wind and the Dove and the Finger of God.

Section 21: *The* testimonium *and the impartation of knowledge*

The *testimonium* is an illumination and a persuasion. It is not an impartation of knowledge. It is the inward side of revelation and therefore can only function as there exists a given objective revelation. It would lose its character as a witness if it were an impartation of knowledge.

For example, it establishes the reality of a canon, but not its limits. The reality of the canon means a truth of God, a giveness of revelation, and its fixation in Scripture. The New Covenant is written, and the life of Christ is documented, and the revelation given the apostles is inscripturated. The reality of a canon is involved in the *testimonium,* for our faith in Scripture is not a matter of critical establishment.[22] Certainly the writers of the New Testament do not establish the Old on critical grounds, but solely on its being the past revelation of God (Heb. 1:1), or the oracles of God (Rom. 3:2). And further, if the canon were settled solely on critical grounds, it would raise afresh the professor-or-Christian issue in a different place. And as Gaussen points out, such a critical establishment of the canon would be purely academic and non-spiritual, and even worse, may be infected with unbelief.[23]

The canon, argues Gaussen, is established by the twofold method of faith and science. It is the *testimonium* which establishes the reality of a canon as spiritual document. James Denney was correct when he wrote: "We do not need to become historical critics before we can believe in Christ and be saved by him. The Holy Spirit, bearing witness by and with the word of the evangelists in our hearts, gives us, independent of any criticism, a full persuasion and assurance of the infallible truth and divine authority of the revelation of God made in him."[24]

22 L. Gaussen, *The Canon of the Holy Scriptures,* p. 418.
23 *Ibid.,* p. 419.
24 *Studies in Theology,* p. 207.

No critical or historical study can deliver to the consciousness of the believer anything but a probable judgment; but only in the *testimonium* do we arrive with certainty at the notion of a written revelation of God.

But the *testimonium* cannot settle the limits of the canon. Here the way of faith must yield to the way of science. "The contention, that the testimony of the Spirit revealed in Christian experience is the test of canonicity," writes de Witt, "is as wide of the mark, and it is an error of the same kind, as the contention that the musical enjoyment of the music of Handel's *Messiah* is testimony to the historical fact that Handel was its author, which is nonsense."[25]

Nor, of course, can textual matters be settled by the *testimonium*. This too would be an impartation of a certain specific bit of knowledge and would force the *testimonium* out of its inward character.

Nor can any specific notion of inspiration be gleaned from the *testimonium* the witness of the Spirit illuminates the mind to the truth of the gospel, and to the divine authority of the documents which contain it. But it does not speak to the origin, mode of writing, or degree of inspiration. The persuasion is a persuasion to truthfulness. It is the simple, direct assent of the mind. But a specific doctrine of inspiration would be a matter of knowledge and therefore would be out of keeping with the structure of the *testimonium*.

Nor is the *testimonium* a voice which says, "The Bible is the Word of God." This would be a revelation, not an illumination. The believer eventually comes to this decision, but not in this manner. He comes at it indirectly through the truth of the gospel. His own life is drawn into the circle of the *testimonium*, and one of the elements in this circle is the divinity and the authority of the written Scripture.

Section 22: *The* testimonium *and the transition*

The New Testament is an open book and may be read by any member of a literate populace. The sentences

25 John de Witt, "The Testimony of the Holy Spirit to the Bible," *The Presbyterian and Reformed Review*, 6:81, 1895.

and propositions are open to all who will take the time merely to read its pages. But no thinking theologian or Christian would identify faith with the ability to read the words of the New Testament and comprehend a measure of their meaning. Reading and comprehending are the prerequisites of faith, for faith comes from hearing and knowing (Rom. 10:17), but they are not faith in themselves. But how does a soul make the transition from comprehending the meaning of the sentences to a saving faith in the meaning of the sentences?

If faith does not come at first, it might be suggested that a more profound search into the meaning of the sentences will arouse faith. But it is too obvious that some of the most learned students of Sacred Scripture have not been believers of its pages; and on the other hand, some very ignorant people have had a very strong faith in the New Testament. What evades the critical scholar seems to come so easily to a very humble and ordinary person. It may be that in certain instances faith has come from a deeper study of the New Testament, or a better acquaintance with the facts surrounding it (e.g., Sir William Ramsay), but the transition generally does not come from an increase of knowledge, or from more precise interpretation, or from additional historical research.

The natural differences among men do not seem to make the difference between faith and unbelief. People with identical mental endowments (whether very intelligent or very ignorant) differ radically among themselves. Scholar opposes scholar, and layman opposes layman. And faith will not come if the scholar attempts to be less than a scholar, or if a layman increases his knowledge. Mental endowment is not the cause of faith nor the root of unbelief.

Wherein, then, stems the transition from knowledge of the documents to faith? How is historical probability changed into saving faith? What is the alchemy which converts the lead of human conviction into the gold of divine confidence? The answer is the *testimonium*. By the *testimonium* historical faith is converted into saving faith, and historical probability into divine certainty. But

again we must be reminded that this is no persuasion
about a document isolated from its content. The documents speak about a certain person, Jesus Christ. And
they speak of a saving relationship created between this
person and believing sinners through faith. This person
takes these believers into a real, mystical, spiritual union
with himself. This persuasion, this mystical union, this
personal presence of Jesus Christ, *are all effected by the
Holy Spirit;* here at this point, and in this manner, is
the transition accomplished.

Therefore the difference among men is the difference
of faith. And faith is a difference made by the Holy
Spirit. Men do not believe because they know more or
less than other men. The difference between faith and
unbelief is the presence or absence of the *testimonium.*
Only the Holy Spirit can make the printed page the Word
of Life; only the Holy Spirit can make the historical
Christ a present person; only the Holy Spirit can make
theological notions saving truths; and only the Holy Spirit
can move the mind out of historical probability into divine certainty.

In connection with the *testimonium* and the transition,
it would be well to examine I Corinthians 12:3 with some
care: "And no one can say 'Jesus is Lord' except by the
Holy Spirit." "Jesus is Lord" is a most remarkable statement. "Jesus" speaks of a certain Jewish person born
about 4 B.C. in Bethlehem, raised in a carpenter's house in
Galilee, and to all external appearances looking no different
from the great multitude of Galileans. He never had the
advantages of position, wealth, or influence which would
have enabled him to advance beyond his fellow men —
whom we judge were somewhat poor and ignorant. The
word "Lord" comes from deep in the Old Testament. It
was one of the customary words of deity. It is true that
the word has many different meanings in the New Testament, not unlike its range of meanings in the English
language itself. But when it is used with reference to
Jesus Christ, it has a very distinct meaning. In a book
completely devoted to the various names ascribed to Jesus,
Vincent Taylor wrote: "Implicit in the recognition of

the lordship of Jesus is the acknowledgment of his essential divinity."[26]

How does the mind make the transition from "Jesus" to "Lord?" Philosophically it appears to be an impossible confusion of the temporal and the eternal, of the omnipresent and the local, of the infinite and the finite, of deity and humanity. Religiously it appears to be either a mythological or a blasphemous statement. Rather than calling for faith it seems to call for a strong repudiation on rational and religious grounds.

Yet unusually rational and religious men — Augustine, Aquinas, Calvin, Luther, Pascal, Leibniz, Berkeley — have said, "Jesus is Lord!" What urged these men to speak — as it would seem — against their rational powers and religious sentiments? The problem of the transition from the Scriptures as a mere book of religion to the Word of Life, and of Jesus to Lord, is the same problem. In fact, they are profoundly interlocked problems.

These men's minds assented and their tongues said "Jesus is Lord" because they were convinced that they were speaking the truth, and that they were saying the truth in a great act of devotion and personal religion. But what is the source of this conviction and of this devotion if it is not the *testimonium?* From the Holy Spirit comes the grace, the light, the power, and the impulse to say "Jesus is Lord!" Certainly it is not our reason that has led us to this point, nor has it been our religious sentiments. As the text states it, *without the Holy Spirit no man can make this confession.*

This truth is foolishness to darkened reason (the Greeks), and a stumblingblock to darkened religious sentiment (the Jews). Neither can admit that "Jesus is Lord." This great reality, this great verity, this great truth, can be said only by a man enlightened and prompted by the Holy Spirit. Those who utter "Jesus is Lord" consider this statement to be truth of very truth. And this truth we have come to possess is so overwhelming in view of its dimensions, and so unlikely in view of our finitude and sinfulness, that we can account for our possession of it only by the *testimonium.* Only by the Holy Spirit can

26 *The Names of Jesus,* p. 51.

we move from the Bible as a book of religion to the Book of God, and only by the Holy Spirit can we move from Jesus the Galilean to "Jesus is Lord!"

Section 23: *Is there a* testimonium *without Scripture?*

The doctrine of the *testimonium* must not be bound too dogmatically to the *written* truth of God. There were times when men had no written Word of God, and certainly the witness of the Spirit cannot be denied them. John Calvin, who sketched out the *testimonium* for the first time in the history of dogmatics, did not exclude the patriarchs from the *testimonium* (IV,viii,5). Abraham had a real evangelical experience of such a nature that he is the pattern of faith for both Gentile and Jew (Rom. 4:11-12). He was justified by faith and without question was regenerated. Therefore he really participated in Jesus Christ. Can Abraham be denied the *testimonium?* There is no ground upon which this may be done. When the Lord of glory appeared to Abraham and called him to leave his homeland, the Spirit of God was working within his heart in such a way that Abraham perceived this call to be the voice of God. And when he believed God and was justified, and exhibited such unbounded faith in the presence of the impossible (Rom. 4:18-21), we cannot doubt that this was accompanied by an inner working of God's Spirit.

When Paul preached to pagans who heard and believed even though they had no Old or New Testament, can it be maintained that they had no *testimonium?* They most assuredly did![27] For the *testimonium* is given in connection with the revelation of God in whatever form it might happen to be. He is the Spirit of truth, and wherever God speaks his truth the Spirit seals it as God's truth. We must gladly admit that in ages where there was no written Word or in conditions where the truth of God was yet in oral form (as in the preaching ministry of Christ and his apostles), or where the truth of

27 John Lawson writes that Irenaeus knew of unlettered tribes who had salvation written in their hearts by the Holy Spirit and were real Christians in the absence of a written record. *The Biblical Theology of Saint Irenaeus*, p. 24.

God in Scripture is known mediately through sermon, song, or Christian literature, *the Spirit yet bears his witness.*[28]

God does not leave us to ourselves in the surety of our salvation, but grants our salvation with a plenitude of certainty. This is the certainty of the *testimonium*, especially in the sense of bearing witness to our sonship, our divine adoption. And from this witnessing emerges our certainty. Whether we have the gospel orally or in print, we are heirs to the same certainty. Therefore, whether we know the truth by sermon, song, or printed page, the Spirit does work and does witness. Certainly there are primitive peoples today who know only the preached Word of God, yet who most assuredly have the *testimonium* within themselves. In our day, if a Christian has any means or ability, he must trace his certainty back to Sacred Scripture; and everything derived from Scripture must in turn be examined on the basis of Scripture.

Section 24: *Are there two* testimonia?

It has been claimed that there are two witnesses of the Holy Spirit: one to the divinity of the Scripture, and one to the divine adoption.[29] The basic motive behind such an assertion is to present a strong, formal validation of the Scripture which is free from any taint of "religious experience." Under the theory of two *testimonia* the full character of the Scripture as the Word of God is not only expressed by the doctrine of the plenary

28 Luke tells Theophilus that he is sending him a *written* life of the Savior to replace the *oral teaching* (*katécheo*, to be orally instructed) that he might have a certain record (Luke 1:1-4). Theophilus, then, must have come to Christ and was instructed in Christian matters by means of oral instruction.

We remind our readers again of the high view of preaching and sacraments held by the Reformers. In them and through them the Word of God came to believing hearts. Preaching to these men was no discussion of religious topics, for the minister was *a minister of the Word of God*, and not a religious specialist as in religious liberalism where the preacher is heard respectfully because he is an educated man.

29 Cf. the entire article by C. W. Hodge, "The Witness of the Holy Spirit to the Bible," *The Princeton Theological Review*, XI (1913), 41-84.

inspiration of Scripture, but also by an intensely Scrip-
ture-centered version of the *testimonium*.

The question may be opened with a look backward to
Calvin, to determine whether the Reformer taught both
a witness to the Scripture, and a separate witness to
divine adoption.[30] Krusche[31] discusses the issue as it has
been raised many times in the history of Protestant theology. He begins by noting that in the *Institutes* Calvin
gives the impression that the *testimonium* is concerned
solely with a formal certification of Scripture as the Word
of God. But Krusche states that this interpretation results
from paying too much attention to the remarks in the
Institutes and not enough to those in the *Commentaries.*
If one properly evaluates Calvin's remarks in the *Commentaries,* he will discover that there is only one witness
in Calvin, not two. In the conclusion of his remarks
Krusche says: "There are not two different witnesses, but
only one . . . Calvin has not separated the certainty of
Scripture from the certainty of salvation as it happened
in orthodoxy. The *testimonium* does not first convince
us of the divine origin of Scripture apart from its content as promise, and then convince us of the content. Both
belong inseparably together [*beides fällt untrennbar in
eins*]."[32] And in another passage Krusche shows how
Calvin has four different facets to the one *testimonium*:
(i) certainty of Scripture: (ii) certainty of salvation:
(iii) certainty of our divine adoption; and (iv) certainty
of the divine authority of the Word which offers the
promise of adoption.[33]

Warfield, another student of Calvin who has given
much attention to his doctrine of the *testimonium,* appears
to say that for Calvin there is but one *testimonium.*
"Given Calvin's general doctrine of the work of the Holy
Spirit in applying salvation, his specific doctrine of the
testimonium Spiritus Sancti in the attestation of Scrip-

30 Hendry indicates that there is in Calvin a formal witness
(the Scriptures are the Word of God) and a material witness (the
content of Scripture, the gospel). *The Holy Spirit in Christian
Theology,* p. 77.

31 Krusche, *op. cit.*, pp. 216ff.

32 *Ibid.*, pp. 217-218.

33 *Ibid.*, p. 263.

ture, and in the applying of its doctrine as well, was inevitable," writes Warfield.[34] And Kuyper, who spent a lifetime studying Calvin, seems specific enough that there is only one witness in Calvin for the certification of the divine authority of Scripture, which is the same as the witness of our adoption. For example, he wrote: "Saving faith is a persuasion, wrought by the Holy Spirit, that the Scripture is a true testimony concerning the salvation of souls, and this salvation includes my soul."[35]

Even if it should be demonstrated that Calvin or certain post-Reformation theologians teach two *testimonia*, there are reasons why we should not readily accede to this doctrine.

(i) There is no clear scriptural evidence for two *testimonia*. That there is a witness to our divine adoption is very obvious from Galatians 4:6 and Romans 8:15-16, but where are there equally clear verses about a distinct testimony concerning Scripture? It is true that I Corinthians 2:1ff. and II Corinthians 3:1ff. could be appealed to for such a separate witness, were it not for the intense christological and soteriological character of these passages. It is our conclusion that the Scriptures fail to present us with the data to establish a double *testimonium*.

(ii) It is obvious that a division in the *testimonium* would represent a great strategic loss. The union of Word and Spirit, with its crystallization in the *testimonium*, is the great bulwark against Romanism, and a *testimonium* about the Scripture separated from the *testimonium* about our divine adoption represents a weakening of this bulwark.

(iii) The thesis that there are two *testimonia* actually calls for a separation of the *form* of Scripture from the *content* of Scripture. Now it is more than certain that we cannot separate the form and the content of Scripture. The main burden of the Scripture is to make us wise unto salvation that is in Jesus Christ (II Tim. 3:15).

34 *Studies in Calvin and Augustine*, p. 72. Cf. also p. 106 and the long section on this theme, pp. 110-112. However, he deems to accept two witnesses in *Critical Reviews*, pp. 233-234. He does not, however, treat the *Commentaries*, where Krusche says the issue is settled.

35 *The Work of the Holy Spirit*, p. 400. Cf. also pp. 192-193, where the two themes are carefully traced out in their unity.

In a real sense the Scriptures are the gospel! Revelation at its acme is the gospel! The Word of God is first the gospel![36]

The person who believes that the purely formal authority of Scripture is the main burden of the *testimonium* is embarrassed by the Bible-believing cultist. What a list of heretics and fanatics can be made of those who believe that the Scriptures are the Word of God! And if we believe in a separate *testimonium* to the formal authority of Scripture separate from the *testimonium* of the divine adoption, we cannot deny them a place next to us. But as soon as the Scripture is joined to its *content* — Jesus Christ and his gospel — then their heresy becomes clear and they have neither the spirit nor the right to stand with us.

This division of one *testimonium* into two goes back deep into Reformed and Lutheran theological history. It was generated by a desire to put Scripture completely and finally over the Church, and to elevate the Bible over everything human, including "religious experience." The result was an interpretation of the *testimonium* exclusively in terms of the divine certification of Scripture. Preiss, for example, claims that when the older Reformed dogmaticians did this, they practically made the Bible a paper pope and were not faithfully reproducing the thought of Calvin.[37] And Preus, whose work is a thorough study of the doctrine of inspiration among the classical Lutheran dogmaticians, affirms that these dogmaticians likewise so emphasized the purely formal validation of Scripture by the *testimonium* that they failed to do justice to the content of Scripture; namely, what it says of Christ, salvation, and assurance.[38]

36 Krusche (*op. cit.*, pp. 256-257) makes much of the point that the Word of God is to Calvin first of all the gospel. That which is the focal point of the witness of the Spirit is the Word of God as gospel. And the center of the gospel is Jesus Christ, or he is the sum of the gospel.

37 Preiss, *op. cit.*, p. 262. It appears at least to me that, if there are two *testimonia*, then we *can* settle the canon by employing the first *testimonium* as a proof-stone for "inspiredness." However, to do this would certainly go against the grain of the entire structure and character of the *testimonium*.

38 R. Preus, *The Inspiration of Scripture*, p. 115.

The notion of two *testimonia* calls not only for a separation of *form* and *content* of Scripture, but also for a separation of the Holy Spirit from Christ. The Holy Spirit, however, is constantly called the Spirit of Christ, which is good Scripture and good theology. As Bromiley states it: "In the Bible and historical theology there is no Pneumatology apart from Christology."[39] And in a study of the Holy Spirit in Paul's writings the same union of christology and pneumatology is strongly emphasized by Wenland.[40] A *testimonium* concerned with the pure validation of Scripture separate from the matter of our adoption thus calls for a work of the Spirit separate from Jesus Christ.

The Scriptures teach one continuum of revelation and salvation, of the oral word and the written word, of the work of Christ and the work of the Spirit. The Spirit, who enables us to see revelation as such (I Cor. 2), is the same Spirit who leads us to say, "Jesus is Lord," (I Cor. 12:3), and who leads us to say, "Abba, Father." It is true that for theological purposes we may speak of the *testimonium* with regard to Scripture, but this is an abstraction necessary for making a particular point. And when we speak of the *testimonium* and our adoption, this, too, is an abstraction from the other aspect of the *testimonium* which enables us to see revelation as revelation, to taste and see Scripture as the Word of God.

(iv) Another complication introduced by two *testimonia* is that there can be no witness to Scripture when revelation is still in oral or traditional form, and therefore something very important for our spiritual life is lost. This theme has already been developed and therefore needs no amplification at this point. Calvin was wiser than his followers, for he did not deny the *testimonium* to those who had no written Scripture. These men "had the testimony of God in their hearts" so that they "knew what they heard was from heaven, and not from earth" (IV,viii,4). If the basic structure of the *testimonium* is the inward illumination of the objective revelation, then

39 G. W. Bromiley, "The Spirit of Christ," *Essays in Christology for Karl Barth*, p. 135.

40 H. Wenland, *op. cit.*, p. 461.

the *testimonium* can exist in full force when the objective revelation is only in oral or traditional form.

(v) Finally, there is a confusion between "religious experience" and the *testimonium*. For example, those who defend two *testimonia* believe that those who have only one confuse the *testimonium* with "religious experience."[41] If we make a distinct *testimonium* for the certification of Scripture to keep it free from religious experience, we are forced to admit that the *testimonium* of adoption is contaminated with religious experience (else why separate them?). Certainly the *testimonium* must be *for* experience. A *testimonium* which is not for experience would be meaningless. Nevertheless the *testimonium* is not religious experience *per se*. The *testimonium* does happen; it does happen to us; it does make a difference; it does alter experience. We cannot flee from experience in any absolute sense, or else the *testimonium* would be like the smile of the cat without the cat. In fact, it is the union of the *form* and *content* of Scripture which saves it from being an abstraction, or a pseudo-decree of an individual Christian playing the role of an ecumenical council. Preiss has stated rather excellently the relationship of the *testimonium* to experience: "And this testimony is really given to us and truly received as a testimony only when all our being receives it. And *precisely because he creates in us a religious experience total and real,* [the Holy Spirit] *cannot be observed adequately by our introspection,* as the fervent adherents of the theology of experience think. And when we speak of it, we cannot describe the secret operation, we only know how to testify to the content of the testimony. It follows that *the Christian will testify less of his experience than of the object of his experience.*"[42]

It can even be asked if there is a *third testimonium*! V. Hepp's doctoral dissertation (*Het testimonium spiritus sancti,* 1914) at the Free University of Amsterdam under the sponsorship of Dr. Bavinck sets up an internal witness of the Spirit to general revelation in exact parallel to special revelation. It has as its christological content

---

41 So C. W. Hodge (*op. cit.,* p. 59) against John de Witt (*op. cit.,* pp. 69-85).

42 Preiss, *op. cit.,* p. 275. Italics are his.

Christ as the spiritual (*asarkikos*) Logos. This has had some acceptance in Holland and America, as witnessed by the favorable discussion in W. Masselink's *General Revelation and Common Grace.*

Krusche (*op. cit.*, pp. 89ff.) examines this view of Hepp, and the views of Gloede, van der Linde, and Engelland, each of which in some way wishes to expand the *testimonium* beyond its strict connection with special revelation and the gospel, and finds them all contrary to Calvin's thought. The *testimonium* in Calvin, reasons Krusche, is restricted to a special form (special revelation) and a special content (Jesus Christ) ; and exactly at those places where we would expect Calvin to speak of a general witness of the Spirit (e.g., in the doctrine of creation, or his doctrine of *semen religionis*) he is silent.

Section 25: *The* testimonium *and some criticisms*

Certain stock arguments often arise against the *testimonium.* For example, there was the Jesuit who held the Bible to his ear pretending to listen for the voice of the Spirit speaking in Scripture, and claiming that he heard nothing. The Protestant can reply merely by placing his ear against the papal throne and declaring that he cannot hear Peter speaking, or against the cornerstone of St. Peter's and claiming that he cannot hear the Church speaking.

Michaelis asserted that he accepted the truths of revelation but never detected such a witness of the Holy Spirit.[43] As it has already been explained, one cannot decipher the structure of the *testimonium* out of his own religious consciousness. The structure is known only from the revelation in Scripture. And there is Strauss's famous statement that the *testimonium* is the Achilles' heel of Protestantism. The Protestant, he reasons, is caught in the dilemma of fanaticism or rationalism.[44] If he takes the witness of the Spirit in all seriousness, he would have

---

43 *Dogmatik*, p. 92. Cited by G. B. Foster, *The Finality of the Christian Religion*, p. 78. And he who tries to *detect* the witness (as Michaelis) or who tries to *feel* the witness (as Foster, p. 70) does not understand the structure of the witness. It is the same order of confusion as trying to feel elect.

44 D. F. Strauss, *Die christliche Glaubenslehre*, I, 136.

to agree with the fanatics that it is complete within itself and does not need the Scripture. But if he follows the rationalists who prove the divinity of Scripture by apologetical means, he does not need the witness of the Spirit. And if he introduces a third thing, the witness of the Spirit coming between the believer and Scripture, then how is he to prove that this third thing is divine? He is caught in an infinite regress, for he needs a divine verification of each preceding supposed divine verification. The best retort is to take Strauss's argument apart, assertion by assertion. Who can take the position of the fanatics seriously? If it is taken seriously, then every proposed utterance of revelation must be accepted as such and the result will be endless theological confusion. The price for this kind of great inward certainty is even greater theological confusion. But if, on the other hand, the fanatic is quietly testing proposed revelations by Scripture, he is tacitly admitting the validity of the *testimonium*. Apologetic arguments, as we have already shown, avail only after illumination, so the rationalistic procedure is also worthless. If the character of the *testimonium* is that of an intuition resulting in a *plērophoria* of the mind, then there is no need for an infinite regress. Once the mind has reached this *plērophoria*, it aquiesces. Further proof of the persuasion could be demanded only if there were some sort of divine aura in the persuasion itself, which is not the case.

The claim of Foster[45] (following Wernle) that modern psychology can explain the *testimonium* as a product of naïve psychology is childish and hardly in keeping with Foster's scholarship. Certainly in 1906 (the date when his book was published) there was enough literature on the subject to caution him against this mistake. Heppe's *Reformed Dogmatics* appeared in 1861; Pannier's dissertation was published in 1893; Klaiber's long essay was published in 1857; and Kuyper's *The Work of the Holy Spirit* was in English in 1900. John de Witt's article in the *Presbyterian and Reformed Review* appeared in 1895. And Foster's notion that the Mohammedans have "the

---

45 Foster, *op. cit.*, p. 78.

same abstract right to appeal to the inner witness of the Spirit" for the Koran will not be taken seriously by anybody who has studied the pneumatology of the Koran.[46]

The most frequent charge of all against the *testimonium* is that the argument is circular: we show the divinity of the *testimonium* by recourse to Scripture, and we show the divinity of Scripture by recourse to the *testimonium*. This was an early charge of the Jesuits against the old Lutheran dogmaticians [47] and has been recently raised by Heim against Calvin[48] and the same Lutheran dogmaticians.[49]

The answer given to Heim by both Krusche (for Calvin) and Preus (for the Lutheran dogmaticians) is essentially the same. The *testimonium* is not the proof of the divinity of Scripture. It is not the *ground* of the authority of Scripture. The Scriptures are *autopistic*, that is, they are in themselves the Word of God. They possess internally their own *indicia* of divinity. The *testimonium* enlightens the eyes of the mind to see this divinity, to apprehend this *autopistia*, to assent to the *indicia*. When Calvin, for example, points out against the enthusiasts that the actions of the Spirit always correspond to the image given of the Spirit in Scripture, he is not doubling back on his argument. He is showing that these supposed revelations of the enthusiasts are not in accord with the image of the Holy Spirit in Scripture. The fanatics or enthusiasts may lay claim to their revelations, but they are not inspired by the Spirit of Sacred Scripture or of Jesus Christ.

The work of the Spirit terminates on the divinity within the Scripture. That this is a divine persuasion is not

46 Foster, *ibid.*, p. 77. C. G. Mylrea (*The Holy Spirit in the Qu'ran and Bible*, 1910) notes that there are twenty references to the Spirit in the Koran. After a study of the commentators on these verses Mylrea comes to the conclusion that they are at a complete loss to make sense out of them. For the most part they are snatched from the Scriptures without any comprehension of their original meaning.

47 Preus, *op. cit.*, p. 110.

48 Krusche, *op. cit.*, pp. 20ff.

49 Preus, *op. cit.*, pp. 111ff. Some scholars admit that the argument is circular but insist that, rather than being a weakness to be regretted, it is the strength of the argument, for it keeps it *spiritual* on both sides. I presume this would be the position of Karl Barth and Otto Weber.

known by the believer by the character or quality of his own inner life but by the revelation in Scripture. To Calvin the Word of God was first the gospel; by faith in it we become God's children, and God sends the Spirit of his Son into our hearts bearing witness that we are his children. This is done in the same breath in which the Spirit illuminates the heart so that it sees the truth of the gospel and embraces it with a *plērophoria* of its truthfulness. Now when the believer turns to Scripture, his mind has been so affected by the Spirit that he can read Scripture for what it is, God's truth. According to Lecerf (who follows Calvin) he sees the *majesty* of God in Scripture; according to Warfield, he sees the divine *indicia;* according to others, he sees the *perfections* of Scripture. But all the objections based on circularity of reasoning fail to see that the divinity perceived is resident in Scripture, and not in some sort of psychic aura of divinity which we experience as the Spirit persuades us.

CHAPTER V

THE *TESTIMONIUM* AND THEOLOGIES

Section 26: *The* testimonium *and Romanism*

When we turn our attention toward Roman Catholicism, we encounter a very strange situation.[1] On the one hand, we discover the Catholic Church teaching that "natural" or "pure" reason, unaided by divine grace, can demonstrate with certainty the existence of God, the spirituality and immortality of the soul, and the divine origin and authority of the Roman Catholic Church. On the other hand, we find Catholic theologians asserting that the evidence within Scripture for its own inspiration is imperfect and incomplete, so that something more than its own self-witness is necessary to bring the mind to a state of certainty about its inspiration. That "something else" is the voice of the teaching *magisterium* of the Roman Catholic Church.

And here is the wonder to behold: (i) The *human mind* by "pure reason"[2] can demonstrate the existence of God and the spirituality and immortality of the human soul. Any conception of faith as an irrational impulse or a blind leap is sternly rebuked by Catholic dogma. So strong is this "pure reason" that it can prove its case beyond a high degree of probability — something most philosophers

1 Cf. *Decrees of the Council of Trent.* Denzinger, *The Source of Catholic Dogma. The Catholic Encyclopedia.* Leo XIII, *On the Holy Spirit* (*Divinum illud,* 1897). *A Catholic Commentary on Holy Scripture.* Ludwig Ott, *Fundamentals of Catholic Dogma.* G. D. Smith, editor, *The Teaching of the Catholic Church.* A. M. Henry, *Introduction to Theology.* Karl Adam, *The Spirit of Catholicism.*

2 Hugh Pope, "Faith," *The Catholic Encyclopedia,* V, 752. This article traces step by step the process of a person from these demonstrations till he stands before the *magisterium* of the Church ready to submit to it. Leo XIII's *Divinum illud* cites many verses on the Holy Spirit but almost completely omits any real interpretation; therefore the significance of these verses is never properly drawn out.

would gladly settle for. It claims to be able to demonstrate these matters in the sense in which logical or geometric theorems are demonstrated.   Even beginners in
philosophy know that since the days of Hume and Kant,
these two subjects (God and the soul) are among the most
controversial in philosophy.   Yet, brushing off modern
philosophy as a passing phase of scepticism in contrast
to Romanism's ageless hold on truth (in this instance,
Thomistic Aristotelianism, which was modernism in its
day), the Catholic theologians claim to drive through,
with no equivocation, to the demonstration of the existence of God and the soul.   What most modern philosophers stumble over, the Catholic philosopher clears with
space to spare.

(ii) Yet, when we turn to what Catholicism terms the
holy, inspired Scripture we are told that the self-witness
of the Bible to its own inspiration is so weak and imperfect, so capable of equivocation, so powerless to speak for
itself, that we cannot be certain of its inspiration until
we are so informed by the Roman Catholic Church.   In
contrast to their bold boasts about pure reason the following statements by Catholic writers about the Scriptures
are spiritually chilling.   The Scriptures are "dead documents," "dead records of primitive documents," "life
grown stiff and numb."   We are told that "the Catholic
does not come to Christ by literary channels, as by the
Scriptural records,"[3] that the Bible is "a dumb and difficult
book,"[4] and that "every biblical scholar knows perfectly
well that there is no book in the world more difficult than
the Bible."[5]   This attitude towards the Scripture is so
much a part of the Catholic apologetics that it could be
documented endlessly.   The human reason can demonstrate
such difficult philosophical matters as the existence of
God and the soul, and that without supernatural help;
whereas the divinely inspired Scriptures are so incomplete and imperfect that their status is really equivocal
until the Church gives its *imprimatur.*

How contrary all of this is to the structure of the

3 Adam, *op. cit.,* p. 50.
4 *A Catholic Commentary on Holy Scripture,* p. 11.
5 M. Sheehan, *Apologetics and Catholic Doctrine,* I, 149.

testimonium, which views with suspicion the power of the human mind to accomplish anything spiritual without the efficacious help of the Holy Spirit; and which teaches that the Scriptures scintillate with a divine luminosity when the heart has been illuminated by the Holy Spirit.

How frightful is the *testimonium* to Catholicism.[6] Catholicism knows the verses which frame the *testimonium* and cites them, and agrees that there is no faith without the grace of the Holy Spirit (*Decrees of the Council of Trent,* Session VI, Chapter V), and that after the act of faith the soul is illuminated with the "light of faith." Yet the biblical structure of the *testimonium* must be weakened by Catholicism, and its great power broken. According to the *testimonium* the Spirit is the adequate and sufficient cause for a profound spiritual certainty, for *plērophoria* of the Christian religion. Through the *testimonium* there is a knowledge of God fully adequate to make the soul wise unto salvation which is in Jesus Christ — the self-witness of Scripture (II Tim. 3:15). Yet Catholicism must *hedge* the power of the Spirit and *darken* the clarity of Scripture to make room for the role of the Church. The Church must add the measure of certainty which the Spirit cannot give in the *testimonium* (which is a biblical doctrine tacitly admitted in the Catholic teaching of "the light of faith") and must add that clarity to the gospel which the Scriptures do not have in themselves.

In a very bold section Karl Adam frankly tells us that the Bible is not adequate in itself. Oral tradition is "prior to and more fundamental than the Bible." Furthermore it possesses a quality which the Bible cannot have because it is a written document. The real power of spiritual persuasion and conviction rests in "the spirit of revelation," in the "mind of the Church." And it is this spirit of revelation which has such a quickening and

6 J. Pannier notes what he calls a curious fact, namely, that the Roman Church, glutted with so many useless things, is extremely poor (*d'une extrême pauvreté*) in its doctrine of the Holy Spirit. *Le Témoignage du Saint-Esprit,* p. 64. In our reading in Catholic literature we encountered no discussion of the implications of I Cor. 2 and II Cor. 3.

persuading power. He comes to this remarkable conclusion: *it is the spiritual guidance and help of the
Church which leads the soul to cry Abba, Father.*[7] Here
is the frank (and to the Protestant, fateful) admission
that the Church displaces the Holy Spirit in the *testimonium.*

In one breath the Roman Church must uphold the
power of human reason to demonstrate certain key religious truths, or else it must capitulate before the sole
power of the Holy Spirit to work any sort of persuasion
in the human heart; and in the next breath it must speak
of the mysterious and incomplete character of Holy
Scripture in order to show its inadequacy as the Spirit's
instrument to create a true knowledge of God in the believer. Yet even this doctrine of natural reason involves
certain unexpected (and certainly vexing) defects. It
is admitted by Catholic theologians that only learned
philosophers are able to prove the existence of God and
the soul, and the divine authority of the Roman Church.
Untrained laymen are disqualified for lack of competence.
But a man may have the requisite philosophical training
and yet be a sceptic like David Hume. The truth, then,
is not obvious to every man who is philosophically competent. In addition to philosophical competence, there
must be added humility. Thus, in reality, just a rela-
tively few Catholic scholars know with certainty the existence of God, the spirituality and immortality of the
soul, and the divine claims of the Roman Catholic Church.
The laymen are disenfranchised because they are not
philosophically competent ("for a great portion of the
human race such a process of scientific demonstration is
a practical impossibility"[8]) ; and those worldly scholars
who reject the proofs are excluded because of their attitude. There is no cure for them save to become humble
and devout in their quest for the truth. But to the in-
competents a sop is handed, known as *prudent conviction.*[9] By following short-cut, popularized versions of
the more sophisticated and involved proofs, the layman
arrives at the same conclusions as the professional phi-

7 *Op. cit.*, pp. 156-157.
8 Smith, *op. cit.*, I, 14.
9 *Ibid.*, I, 14, 15.

losopher; but because he did not follow through step by step he cannot enjoy their certainty of demonstration but must remain satisfied with prudent conviction. And for the layman this is adequate. *But it must not be overlooked that only the philosopher really knows; that only the philosopher has unalloyed certainty; and that according to Catholic premises only the philosopher has a valid motivation to seek the Church,* for the entire structure of the Preamble of the Faith is to show how a man is motivated to look for the truth in the Roman Catholic Church.

When we discussed the "professor or Christian" issue in a previous section, we noted there how the *testimonium avoids* these problems of the Catholic procedure. By virtue of the *testimonium* the humblest person enjoys the same certainty as the learned theologian. Is it not a very unchristian procedure to exalt natural reason to the point where it can clearly demonstrate the Preamble of Faith; and to depress the witness of the Scripture to the point where its witness is equivocal unless rescued by the testimony of the Church?

It is not difficult to understand why the Catholic Church must brand the *testimonium* as subjectivism, and why it must weaken all those passages which speak of the Holy Spirit giving the believer a divine assurance of the faith; it is because the final word of assurance must be given by the Church. The Reformation issue is here in all its force: the Lord, the Holy Spirit, gives a divine testimony to the gospel and the Word of God; or, the voice of man speaking *ex cathedra* gives a human opinion about a divine matter. Is it not frightening that the voice of man is given a greater assuring power than that of the divine barrister, the Holy Spirit?[10]

10 We call attention to the passage in Smith (*op. cit.*, I, 170), in which the *testimonium* is specifically rejected and is replaced by the Roman Catholic *magisterium* which speaks *exactly* as God speaks. But he has not shown that the *testimonium* is not in Scripture itself; nor has he shown that the Holy Spirit speaking in the heart *is not a divine voice* spoken by a divine Person and therefore with the authority of God. At least one Catholic writer has seen the measure of truth in the inner work of the Holy Spirit, but unfortunately tries to keep his feet dry by saying that the individual's personal experience of the Holy Spirit must not go contrary to the unity of the Church. Henry, *op. cit.*, I, 17-18.

Calvin saw through certain of the difficulties with the Catholic position which are still valid today. To begin with, Calvin believed that the pope, the Mohammedans, and the fanatics were all guilty of the same mistake, namely, that of taking the Spirit *without* the Word as the sign of the Church. This he pointed out with force and clarity to Sadolet in his famous *Reply*. Calvin reasoned that because the Spirit is invisible, the Church must be directed by something tangible and public — Sacred Scripture. The sign of the true Church, then, is that it governs itself by the Word of God, whereas in Catholicism the teaching *magisterium* of the Church is identified with Jesus Christ and the Holy Spirit. On these premises (as Karl Barth has shown in modern times) the Roman Church carries on a conversation within herself. There is no provision for God speaking a word of correction, judgment, or reformation to her. But the Church can purify herself only as she listens, not as she speaks; only as she hears, not as she decrees. When the locus of the teaching of the Spirit is the *magisterium* of the Church and not the Word of God, there can be no reforming word of God spoken to the Church and the Roman Church follows the theological meandering of its hierarchy.

There is another important criticism of Calvin which points out the disadvantageous position of the Church to impart a true spiritual certainty. The Church is "at a distance" from the human spirit. People are persuaded by books (literature) or by other people. But books and people are *exterior* to the human spirit, i.e., they are "at a distance." Their powers to persuade are strictly limited and circumscribed. But the Church, too, is exterior, "at a distance," to the human spirit and this Calvin

11 We commend William Shaw Kerr's *Handbook on the Papacy* as a carefully documented and frank discussion of these matters. Deep into the twentieth century Catholic authors have defended the rights of force, torture, and death for heretics. See the four chapters on "Persecution," "The Inquisition," "The Spanish Inquisition," and then the heart-breaker on "Galileo." The serious rethinking of this matter among Catholics along with a defense of religious liberty upon Catholic premises is set forth by A. F. Carrille de Albernez in "Roman Catholicism and Religious Liberty," *Ecumenical Review*, XII (1959), 23-43. What is missing in this article, however, is any reference to the use of *force*.

considers a very weak position. *That is why the Catholic Church has had to use the sword, the torture chamber, the inquisition, and the jail to persuade.*[11] Only the Holy Spirit is the interior, the ethical, the spiritual persuader.

Calvin did not reject the Church, and Catholicism does not reject the Holy Spirit. But to Calvin the Church *directs* us to the truth and helps us along to it; the final persuasion comes from the *testimonium*. Romanism does believe that saving faith is possible only by the grace of the Holy Spirit, but certainty comes from the infallible teaching *magisterium* of the Roman Church giving the Catholic believer "passive infallibility." But in Calvin's doctrine the persuader is in the right place — in the heart, in the spirit; whereas in Catholicism the Church is "at a distance," and therefore is in no position to persuade efficaciously. By remaining faithful to the biblical theme that the believer has "the witness within himself" (I John 5:10), Calvin is closer to the teaching of the apostles than are the Catholics, who believe essentially in an external persuasion.

There remains yet another point of the Catholic position that must be treated. According to Catholic theologians a competent philosopher, with requisite humility, can prove the existence of God and the spirituality and immortality of the soul. This brings to his mind the general topic of religion, so he inquires about various religions. He encounters the Bible, which he understands well enough with his reason to note that it talks about a church. He must now inspect churches. Once again by following reason he decides that the Roman Catholic Church is the true Church of Jesus Christ. Then he learns of the claims of the Church. So by following the road of pure reason he starts "from scratch" and eventually discovers himself standing before the priest and altar in a cathedral. But he is not yet a *Christian*. He has come to this point by natural reason. *What is the actual, concrete decision now before him?* It is whether he should submit *to the Roman Catholic Church, its magisterium, and its creed.* He is not confronted directly with the Word of God, with the gospel, or with Jesus Christ. He is directly confronted with the Roman Catholic Church, her hierarchy, and her claims.

According to Calvin the sinner is confronted with the person of Christ, with the gospel, with the Word of God. *And it is in this context that the Spirit works.* Thus it is obvious, at least to an evangelical Protestant, that in the Catholic Church the Church displaces Christ, his gospel, and the Word of God. We get to Christ and his benefits by first submitting to the *magisterium* of the Church. Thus the total biblical structure of objective and subjective revelation, the union of Word and Spirit, is fractured.

According to Romanism the Protestant position is subjectivism. Romanism does not deny the illumination of the believer by the Spirit, but believes that if it is made the sole principle of religious knowledge, then it is subjectivism. In reply it may be said:

(i) The *testimonium* is universal in principle. It is the right of every believer, and the potential gift to every person who will believe. It is as universal as the intentions of the gospel and as widespread as the extension of the Christian Church. As far as each believer is concerned, he believes that the principle possesses universal validity.

(ii) The *testimonium* is not mysticism. It is not an ineffable experience in which the human spirit mystically unites with the divine Spirit. Rather, it is the divine Spirit *acting upon* the human spirit. The consciousness of the believer is not directed toward the union as such, but toward the content of the gospel, about which he can give *effable* testimony.

(iii) The *testimonium* is anchored in the events of history, and transcribed in Scripture. It is a witness about Jesus Christ: his death, his resurrection, his ascension. As Bromiley[12] remarks, although the Spirit accomplishes a subjective realization of salvation, the test of this working is not subjectivism because this would call for a separation of the Spirit from Jesus Christ. It is a witness founded upon the outpouring of the Holy Spirit in the day of Pentecost: a definable time, a definable place, and a known company of men. Its entire structure is publicly set down in the New Testament.

12 "The Spirit of Christ," *Essays in Christology for Karl Barth,* p. 140.

(iv) The *testimonium* is subjective in the sense that everything which requires a certain perceptivity, or a decision, is subjective. Even the claims of Romanism must be subjectivized through decision. Great art, great poetry, and great music are all subjective insofar as they require a certain perceptivity for their proper appreciation. But this is not subjectivism in the pejorative sense. When we say that only the pure in heart see God, this is not subjectivism. We simply state a subjective qualification for encountering a great objective reality, God. And so the *testimonium* deals with the subjective dimension of the great objectivity of the gospel of Jesus Christ.

(v) The person who undergoes the *testimonium* in almost every instance finds himself associated with other Christians. Regardless of different racial, national, or cultural origins he finds a common denominator in the gospel of Christ. It is true that the *testimonium* cannot be objectified but: (a) its content may be objectified — the gospel; and, (b) like Paul, those who have undergone illumination may recount their personal experiences. Thus a common feeling, a sympathy of faith, a harmony of belief, a rapport of spirit exists among Christians which, while not an objectification of the *testimonium*, constitutes an *objectifying witness* to the reality of the *testimonium*.

The Catholic theory confronts the Protestant with the problem of natural reason, which in Protestantism is best stated as the problem of Christian evidences. It may be framed as follows: Should the evidences of the Christian faith (e.g., prophecy, miracles, the resurrection of Christ, the greatness of the truths of the Bible, the suitability of its doctrines, etc.) be part of the Christian preaching in its attempt to appeal to man's natural reason, or should evangelistic preaching confine itself solely to the gospel?

This problem has a long history and is still much debated today. Calvin, in his *Institutes*, followed his discussion of the *testimonium* (I,vii) immediately with a chapter on rational proofs (I,viii). Calvin scholars are still much agitated about the proper relationship between these two chapters. Nevertheless, three major opinions are found among Reformed and Lutheran scholars on the question of evidences:

(i) One group believes that the evidences ought to be preached. They may create *historical faith* in the mind of the sinner, which is not a long step from saving faith. Thus evidences give a provisional or probable certainty which is made full and complete by the gospel. Either men still have enough reason left undamaged by sin to assent to the proofs, or common grace overcomes their sinfulness so that they may assent to the proofs.

(ii) Another group believes that the Spirit does not create a blind faith. Evidences in themselves cannot create faith, for faith comes only by the action of the Spirit. But the Spirit works in conjunction with evidences. The evangelist must give good reasons for becoming a Christian; and if the reliability or credibility of certain matters be questioned, he must give an adequate defense. Thus if the Spirit illuminates the mind of the sinner, he will immediately see the credibility of the evidences.

(iii) A third group believes that only the gospel ought to be preached to sinners. The Spirit works only with the calculus of sin, death, judgment, righteousness, Christ, the cross, and forgiveness; not with reasons, proofs, or demonstrations of various sorts. Therefore evangelistic preaching must confine itself to Christ and omit evidences. After a person believes, then he may investigate Christian evidences and find that they substantiate his faith. But the third group takes almost a cavalier attitude toward evidences. The witness of the Spirit is so impressive and so autonomous that evidences appear almost as inconsequential.

In our judgment the first position must be considered defective. Only the Holy Spirit may efficaciously persuade a blind and rebellious heart, and therefore the attempt to create an historical faith and provisional certainty by the preaching of evidences cannot succeed. The second and third positions may not be as far apart as they appear; however, the third group has no right to take a cavalier attitude toward Christian evidences.

The *testimonium* is a certification of our personal adoption. But Christianity is also an objective religion of God. Christian evidences are to objective religion what the *testimonium* is to personal religion. That is why there is an emphasis in the prophets on the value of fulfilled prophecy, and an emphasis in the New Testament on the significance of miracles. The *testimonium* validates one's personal participation in redemption; evidences validate the objective religion of the gospel. A cavalier treatment of Christian evidences is therefore a failure to understand the total complex of the Christian revelation.[13]

Section 27: *The* testimonium *and religious liberalism*

It is not unusual to find a theologian of the school of religious liberalism approaching the *testimonium* like a Caleb approaching Hebron and saying, "Give me that mountain!" In religious liberalism there is a subjectivizing of religion; and so far as the *testimonium* has to do with the subjectivizing of revelation, it appears that the religious liberals' understanding of religion and the *testimonium* were made for each other. So men like Sabatier gladly take to themselves the Reformers' doctrine of the *testimonium*.[14]

But they do not take the Reformers' doctrine in its entirety. The Reformers were children of their times, they say, and framed this doctrine accordingly. Modern science and modern biblical criticism had not yet freed them from certain traditional presuppositions. The Reformers, nevertheless, saw the truth in its essence, namely, *the autonomy of religious experience as such; the evi-*

13 Klaiber, "Die Lehre der altprotestantischen Dogmatiker von dem *testimonium spiritus sancti,* und ihrer dogmatischen Bedeutung," *Jahrbücher für Deutsche Theologie,* II/1, pp. 1-54, 1857, discusses the beliefs of the older Lutheran dogmaticians about this point. Many of them would be in group (i). Warfield is very strong in defending position number (ii). Cf. *Calvin and Augustine,* pp. 84ff. Kuyper was close to position (iii), as is evident from the sharp division of Warfield and Kuyper on this subject, which is apparent in Warfield's review of Kuyper's opinions in Warfield's preface to Beattie's *Christian Apologetics.* Warfield sturdily classifies Calvin in group (ii). Most recent scholarship puts Calvin in group (iii). Cf. Niesel, *The Theology of John Calvin,* p. 37, n. 1.

14 Auguste Sabatier, *Religions of Authority and the Religion of the Spirit,* pp. 160ff., throughout Book III.

dential value of religious experience; the unimpeachable authority of Spirit touching spirit free from any external compulsion of Church or Book.

Being children of their times, the Reformers still adhered to certain views about the Bible and to certain scholastic views of the character of theology, but for this they are gladly forgiven. Their successors, however, lost the insight which the Reformers had into the autonomy of religious experience, and perpetuated only their views of Scripture and dogma. But even their perpetuating was not wholly faithful, but narrowing, dogmatizing, and formalizing. Developing their dogmatics in divergence from the spirit of the Reformers, they produced that leadened monstrosity known as "Protestant scholasticism." Thus the Reformed and Lutheran Churches, having been freed from the authoritarianism of Rome, became enslaved once more by an authoritarianism which in its own way was worse than that of Rome. The Roman Church is at least a living, moving, sensitive corporation which can adapt its thought and life to the changing times. But the authoritarianism of the Bible leaves the Church saddled with a dead book whose truth is frozen in ancient thought categories which must be callously imposed upon modern man.

However, thanks to Schleiermacher, say the liberals, the insight of the Reformers was recovered and the deadening influence of scholastic orthodoxy was broken. The significance of the *testimonium* was recovered: it speaks to the reality of the life of God in the soul of man; of the feeling of filial piety which creates an unshakeable inner assurance of the fatherhood of God; of the autonomy of the spirit of Jesus in the life of believers, freeing them from all oppressive authoritarianism; of the power of the Bible to witness to the reality of religious experience and to stimulate contemporary readers to relive these experiences in their own lives. This view contrasts sharply with the "authority of a priest or a book" which "inevitably becomes a yoke which either weighs down the human being or urges him to revolt."[15]

Now if Catholicism is the Church conversing with it-

15 *Ibid.*, p. 262.

self as we have shown above, then religious liberalism is the involution of this error. It is *man's spirit talking with itself*. In both instances there is no magisterial Word of God spoken and heard. Barth writes in his own "Barthian" way: "Modernist thought hears man answer without anyone having called him. It hears him talk to himself."[16] It is the same error of the enthusiasts and fanatics of the Reformation, who equated the deliveries of man's own spirit with the revelation of God; who divorced the Spirit from the Word; who tipped their hats politely to the Bible, but ignored its *magisterium*.

In reality, there is no *testimonium* in religious liberalism. To begin with, the *testimonium* is God speaking into the darkness and blindness and sinfulness of the human heart (II Cor. 4:3ff.). But there is no radical doctrine of sin in religious liberalism to which the *testimonium* relates itself. There is only sensuousness or spiritual torpidity or religious indifference or a dormant religious potentiality.

There is no Trinity in religious liberalism. There is then no Father who speaks; no Son who mediates; and no Spirit who acts. In the *testimonium* God the Holy Spirit, a divine person, bears his witness, and this divine person is no mere synonym for the immanence of God. Religious liberalism has no doctrine of the Holy Spirit adequate to the *testimonium*.

There is no incarnation in religious liberalism. According to its christology Jesus Christ represents the highest potentiality of man's religious nature. Having raised this potentiality to its perfection, he becomes the founder of the Kingdom and the Church. But the *testimonium* is concerned with a confession of Jesus as the divine Lord (I Cor. 12:3), as incarnate God. The denial of the incarnation is *not a mark of the Spirit of God, but of the spirit of antichrist* (I John 4:1ff.).

There is no divine salvation in religious liberalism. There is only arousal of religious potential, a rooting up of spiritual subsoil, the forming of a religious consciousness. There is no God who by the incarnation takes our

16 *Church Dogmatics*, I/1, p. 68.

cause upon himself; no theanthropic person who goes to the cross and takes our judgment and contradiction upon himself, who goes through death and emerges risen from the dead to share with us his victory over the grave. And the *testimonium* is one of the important facets of the subjective application of this divine salvation.

There is no supernaturalism in religious liberalism. On the contrary, it is a very concerted effort to eliminate everything supernatural from the Christian faith. But the *testimonium* is a major piece of biblical supernaturalism. It is a power which comes upon the soul from without; it is the accomplishment of that which we cannot accomplish ourselves. The great French Reformed theologian Doumergue cried out: "The Holy Spirit is God, and not we ourselves. What we are speaking of is a Spirit which illuminates our spirit, which purifies our spirit, which strives against our spirit, which triumphs over our spirit. And you say this Spirit is nothing but our spirit? By no means. The Holy Spirit, the Spirit of God — this is God coming into us, not coming from us."[17]

There is no Word of God in the Scriptures of religious liberalism and therefore no *testimonium*. The Scriptures (in religious liberalism) have been changed from the document of revelation to a record of religious experiences. The Scriptures have ceased to be the *magisterium* of God and have become subject to the criticism of men. Thus, in religious liberalism, rather than a binding to the Word of God, there is a criticism of the Word of God. Sabatier wrote: "Moses, Isaiah, Paul, John, Peter, are to me and will continue to be, in the religious order, men of God clothed with a very great moral authority; I put myself to school to them, I profit by their lessons, they are incomparable models and precious teachers; but, after all, *I am still free to choose between their ideas, to criticize their reasonings, to reject such of their teachings as are to me unassimilable.*"[18] But the *testimonium* calls for an assent to the truths of revelation (I Cor. 2:1ff.), and a

17 Cited by Warfield, *Calvin and Augustine*, p. 111.
18 *Op. cit.*, p. 264. Italics mine. Warfield says it is odd for religious liberalism to claim the *testimonium* when one of its chief tenets is a rejection of the authority of Scripture, one of the major intentions of the *testimonium*. *Op. cit.*, p. 125.

binding to the terms of the New Covenant (II Cor. 3 :1ff.),
which in turn binds to the document of the Covenant, the
New Testament.

The religious liberals do not have the *testimonium* because they relate it improperly to religious experience.
Just as revelation generates Scripture, the *testimonium*
generates experience; but religious experience is not
identical with the *testimonium*. The *testimonium* generates a sense of divine sonship, but the sense of sonship is
a result, not a cause (which the *testimonium* is). Liberalism betrays its betrayal of the *testimonium* when its
writers speak so uniformly of it as a *feeling*. But this
is not what the *testimonium* produces; it produces rather
a *plērophoria* about Jesus Christ, his gospel, and the documents which contain it.

There is only one conclusion we may draw: there is no
testimonium in religious liberalism.

Section 28: *The* testimonium *and fundamentalism*

Contrary to many recent analyses of fundamentalism,
it is not a simple movement to define. There is a uniform
tendency to judge the movement by its more vocal repre-
sentatives, and even at that, by their controversial utter-
ances alone. There are many soft-spoken saints among
the fundamentalists, and these people of God exhibit a
great spirit of consecration and dedication to Jesus Christ.
They are people of prayer, of sacrificial giving, and of
fervent serving. In developing such emphases as are
found in the victorious life movement (or deeper life
movement), they have developed a warm, spiritual tradition which seldom makes the pages of controversial jour-
nalism. Here we have unmistakable pressure from the
side of the Holy Spirit.

But fundamentalism does not treat the *testimonium* in
a satisfactory and sustained manner. These brethren
have written books on the Holy Spirit and reveal acquaintance with the existence of the *testimonium,* but the *testimonium* (as developed by the Reformers) is always on
the periphery. This does not mean that there is no *testimonium* among the fundamentalists. They are believers
and therefore share in the *testimonium.* The Spirit is
faithful to himself and to his revelation, and even those

people who do not have a proper comprehension of the structure of the *testimonium* enjoy the *testimonium* itself. But fundamentalism has not truly interacted with the *testimonium* and therefore, while fervent in its doctrine of the Holy Spirit, it is usually deficient in its evaluation of the *testimonium*. Not being grounded properly in the *testimonium*, it replaces it functionally with a pietistic religious testimony.

Why has fundamentalism failed with respect to the *testimonium?* The diagnosis of this phenomenon calls for patient, serious, selfless conversation between Christian brothers. It calls for a fresh examination of Scripture in Berean fashion to see if these things be so. The error of fundamentalism is nothing like that of Catholicism, which freezes the Holy Spirit in the Church and its hierarchy, nor of liberalism, whose presuppositions make the *testimonium* impossible; rather, it is the result of an imperfect and incomplete interaction with the *testimonium*.

First, fundamentalism represents a narrowing of the Christian faith in every dimension: theologically, educationally, socially, and culturally. The full account of this narrowing is a story in itself. One of the aspects of this narrowing is that fundamentalism was so concerned to defend the inspiration of the Scriptures against all liberals outside the camp and all concessionists within the camp that it lost track of the more comprehensive doctrine of revelation. It spoke much of the "inspired Word of God" but forgot the priority of the "revealed Word of God." In this narrowing process it then lost its heritage of a great doctrine of revelation. It failed to grasp the truth that inspiration lives on revelation and not vice versa. Nothing was so telltale at this point as the fundamentalists' inability to launch an effective attack upon the views of revelation propounded by Brunner and Barth. For the most part their polemic against neo-orthodoxy is limited to sniping attacks on the neo-orthodox view of inspiration.

Whenever and wherever the larger structure of revelation is lost and the conception of the nature of Scripture is greatly narrowed, there is no profound insight into the *testimonium*, for the *testimonium* derives its foundation and strength from a comprehensive view of revelation.

Second, fundamentalism in fiercely defending the Scripture against modernism lost the perspective of the instrumental character of Scripture, and gave Scripture an independent life of its own. Modernism was without doubt a denial of the inspiration and authority of Scripture; but a general must not let the heat of one battlefront govern his total strategy. If he rushes his troops into one sector and drains his supplies into another area, he will shortly find himself overexposed and undersupplied at other places where he can ill afford it. Fundamentalism poured its troops into battle for the rights of Scripture without carefully checking its heritage of dogmatics, and soon began to attribute an independent power and life to Scripture — a power and life which Reformed dogmaticians from Calvin on reserved for the Holy Spirit. Thus among fundamentalists the expression "the Word" became theologically equivalent to the expression "Word and Spirit" among Reformed theologians.

But if one gives Scripture this independent life and power, what happens to the *testimonium?* Are the assertions of Scripture about its own power to be isolated from those assertions about the Holy Spirit? If so, the *testimonium* is displaced. Calvin taught that Scripture is the instrument whereby the Spirit illuminates our minds, and that without the Spirit the Word is "only a clang which disturbs the air and strikes our ear, but does not press into our hearts, for the Spirit has not created an internal entrance for the Word."[19] Furthermore, Calvin did not assign any magical powers to the Scripture, no ontological inspired quality which could affect a man's heart without the presence of the Holy Spirit; rather, it was the incomparable message of the Sacred Scripture which constituted its fitness to be employed as the instrument of the Holy Spirit.[20] In not keeping close to the Reformed doctrine at this point, and in losing sight of the concept of Scripture as the instrument of the Spirit, the fundamentalists ended up with a sacramental view of Sacred Scripture, a kind of *ex opere operato* of the printed word. When they remembered the *testimonium,* they gave

19 Krusche, *op. cit.,* p. 224; cf. *Institutes,* IV, xiv, 8.
20 *Ibid.,* p. 182.

it a polite acknowledgment, but they never gave it a real place because their sacramental view of Scripture made it a duplication. Fundamentalism needs to hear the words of Kuyper: "Not, of course, as though that Bible by itself were sufficient to give to every one who reads it, the true knowledge of God. We positively reject such a mechanical explanation and by their teaching of the witness of the Holy Spirit as absolutely indispensable for all *conviction* concerning the Scripture, by their requirement of illumination for the *right understanding* of the Scripture and by their high esteem of the ministry of the Spirit for the *application* of the Scripture, our fathers have sufficiently shown that such a mechanical explanation cannot be ascribed to them."[21] Kuyper uses the word "mechanical" in the sense that we have used the word "sacramental."

Third, the fundamentalists never realized how much they were children of the scientific era. Under great pressure for a sort of scientific respectability (greater than they are willing to admit), they let the spirit of science permeate their apologetics. If the inspiration of the Scriptures could be *scientifically* demonstrated, several wonderful things would be accomplished: (i) the modernist view of the Bible would be discredited; (ii) unbelief could be easily branded as irrational; and (iii) the mighty voice of science would stand on the side of orthodoxy.

Consequently apologists of such conviction looked for Einsteinian space in Genesis 1, a theory of matter in Hebrews 11:3, or anticipations of modern physics and chemistry in Exodus or Leviticus. Wherever and whenever they were found — and they were found! — they were claimed as scientific proofs of inspiration. Or better yet, if inspiration could be pinned down with a sort of mathematical proof, then inspiration was really demonstrated. Nothing was more up to date than fundamentalism, for it had Heisenberg and Einstein on its side.

But when apologetics is conceived so rationally and scientifically (and unspiritually), where is the place for the *testimonium?* If an unbeliever could be effectively

21 Kuyper, *Principles*, p. 360. Italics are his.

disarmed by a verse anticipating Einstein, what need for the *testimonium?* It is more than evident that in developing this sort of scientific apologetics, fundamentalism could not properly interact with the *testimonium.*

This is the story of some of its leaders, but not of the total movement. A number of lesser-known men, although not schooled in Reformed theology, stood for the equivalent of the *testimonium.* This was manifest in their devotional literature; in the choruses they wrote; in their desire to be Spirit-filled; and in the literature they produced against Pentecostalism. However, the inability of the leaders of fundamentalism to incorporate the *testimonium* properly into their apologetics and theology was a manifest symptom that fundamentalism represented a serious narrowing of the Christian faith. The narrow version of Christianity which it did defend had its root in Reformed theology, but it underwent some unlovely changes when it was torn from the trunk.

Section 29: *The* testimonium *and Kierkegaard and Pascal*

There is no evidence that Kierkegaard read a word of Pascal, yet scholars find a spiritual affinity between the two men. They both reacted against a rationalistic approach to the Christian faith. Pascal was unhappy with Descartes, whom he accused of politely acknowledging the existence of God and then proceeding in his philosophy as if God did not exist. He was also most disturbed with the sceptical Frenchmen who were so worldly-wise but incredibly irrational about things eternal. Kierkegaard was perturbed with the efforts of some of his fellow Danes who were trying to hegelianize Christianity, so that to be a Christian meant no more than to think philosophically. He also greatly opposed the concept of the state Church, which permitted a Dane to be a church member with none of the New Testament elements of decision, suffering, and cross-bearing. His *Attack on Christianity* is sharp, clever, and ruthless. Both men opposed the theistic proofs, for these proofs attempted to speak of God independently of the spirit of worship, devotion, and suffering for the name of Jesus Christ which is characteristic of New Testament religion.

Both men wrote with great penetration into the char-

acter of Christian experience, based not upon scientific
exegesis of the New Testament but upon a serious, in-
tensive, spiritual study of the New Testament. Each
attempted to sketch that series of inward steps whereby
a man comes into a transforming experience of the gospel.
Pascal taught a doctrine of the *intuitive mind,* which
meant a direct apprehension of reality, in contrast to the
geometric mind which grasped things rationally and ex-
ternally. In the religious realm the intuitive mind is the
heart, and the mistake of the apologists is to present the
Christian faith to the geometric mind rather than to the
heart. When a man apprehends the Christian faith by
the heart, he undergoes a profound, even mystical, experience. Kierkegaard's view was similar. Matters of fact
are grasped by the method of *approximation,* which involves no passion or decision. But when man lays hold
of the gospel by the method of *appropriation,* by spirit
(redefined by Kierkegaard to mean that part of man which
mediates time and eternity — an existentialist notion),
then the faith is grasped in passion, inwardness, subjectivity. And thereby the human spirit is spirituality
raised to its acme.

How the thought of these two men is to be related to
the *testimonium* is very important. The critical point is
just how these psychological expositions are to be understood. For example, if they are designed for a kind of
psychological sparring with men who fail to apprehend
truly the nature of the Christian faith, or with men who
see no relevance of the gospel to themselves, then these
expositions might be judged as a kind of apologetics. Not
ordinary apologetics, but shrewd psychological apologetics.
Both men were like sharp boxers attempting to put fast
jabs through the presumed airtight defense of their opposition. The sting of their blows was intended to
awaken men to the reality of the Christian gospel which
for one reason or another was not considered as a relevant
option. Their writings might be compared to the writings
of C. S. Lewis in our time. And certainly there is a need
in every generation for a few non-conformist apologists
to jab effectively at the sophistication or spiritual indifference of their contemporaries.

Or, rather than being non-conformist apologists, they

might be serious students of the psychology of religion. Regeneration is strictly God's action and it is studied from a distinctly theological orientation. But there are psychological components in regeneration as it effects conversion, and this may be a proper subject matter of study. The Christian theologian must say something about religious psychology when he discusses regeneration and conversion, just as he must say something about history and sociology when he discusses the Church. And we cannot deny the right of men like Augustine, Pascal, Newman, or Kierkegaard to attempt to sketch the inward pilgrimage of the soul as viewed from the perspective of the prodigal.

But if these structures of Pascal and Kierkegaard are psychological substitutes for the *testimonium,* then they must be judged adversely. If these theories affirm that there is a powerful spiritual potential in man (spirit — existentially defined; or, heart) which if properly triggered produces a great spiritual transformation of the soul, then they stand in direct competition with the *testimonium.* They are but a psychological *ex opere operato,* and therefore represent the same kind of error as the funamentalists' *ex opere operato* Scripture.

The *testimonium,* unfortunately, is not discussed by Pascal or Kierkegaard, although the writings of both contain a strong evangelical note; and certainly both men would be quick to recognize the central importance of the Holy Spirit. However, the danger of Kierkegaard and Pascal is that their psychological doctrines threaten to displace the *testimonium.* One cannot identify the *testimonium* with either Kierkegaard's method of appropriation or Pascal's doctrine of the heart. And the danger is that subsequent existentially minded theologians will be tempted to displace the *testimonium* with an existential substitute.[22] The regeneration of the heart, the illumination of the mind, and the realignment of the will must always be attributed to the action of the Spirit of God.

22 An approximation of this may be found in Otto Weber's treatment of the *testimonium* (*Grundlagen der Dogmatik,* I, 266-273, "Testimonium Spiritus Sancti internum"). The discussion follows Kierkegaard's notion of the believer becoming contemporary with

Christ (p. 272). Barth's doctrines of the Word of God coming to a contemporary speaking and hearing, and that the inspiration of the Scripture is no resident quality of the Scriptures, but that the Scriptures are an authentic witness to revelation, are also advocated. The *testimonium* is the freedom of the Holy Spirit so acting that the believer comes to a hearing of the Word of God with a call to obedience and decision; wherein the believer *hears* and *answers;* wherein the believer meets Jesus Christ through the word of Scripture. There is no objective criterion for the proof of the existence of the Word of God in Scripture. Both the Word and the Content are spiritual, for *"Schriftevidenz und Geistesbezeugnis sind 'identisch.' "* (p. 268). The so-called circle of the *testimonium* is not to be avoided but freely confessed. Only a foolish apologetic will attempt to avoid it. The traditional doctrine is represented, unfortunately, in a rather poor light, i.e., it is based almost exclusively upon the so-called scholastic Protestant dogmaticians and presented as a sort of supernatural verification of verbal inspiration.

SELECTED BIBLIOGRAPHY

ATHANASIUS. *The Letters of Athanasius concerning the Holy Spirit.* Translated by C. R. B. Shapland. London: The Epworth Press, 1951. This book is historically important as it represents the point at which the *homoousian* was applied to the Holy Spirit.

BARTH, KARL. *Kirchliche Dogmatik.* Zollikon-Zürich: Evangelischer Verlag, 1948. I/2, "Die Lehre vom Wort Gottes," Section 16, "Die Freiheit des Menschen für Gott," is Barth's version of the *testimonium.*

————. *The Holy Ghost and the Christian Faith.* London: Frederick Muller, 1938.

BROMILEY, G. W. "The Spirit of Christ," *Essays in Christology for Karl Barth.* Edited by T. H. Parker. London: Lutterworth Press, 1956.

CALVIN, JOHN. *Institutes of the Christian Religion.* 2 vols. Translated by John Allen. Grand Rapids: Wm. B. Eerdmans, 1949. This contains the classical statement of the *testimonium.*

————. *Theological Treatises. The Library of Christian Classics,* Vol. XXII. Philadelphia: The Westminster Press, 1954.

————. *Tracts Relating to the Reformation.* 3 vols. Edinburgh: Calvin Translation Society, 1954.

CUNNINGHAM, WILLIAM. *Theological Lectures.* New York: Robert Carter, 1878.

DAVIES, RUPERT E. *The Problem of Authority in the Continental Reformers.* London: The Epworth Press, 1946. This contains an exposition of the views of Luther and Calvin.

DEVIVIER, W. *Christian Apologetics.* 2 vols. New York: F. Wagner, 1924. This is a standard work on Catholic apologetics.

ELERT, WERNER. *Der christliche Glaube.* Dritte Auflage. Hamburg: Furche Verlag, 1956.

GAUSSEN, L. *The Canon of the Holy Scriptures from the Double Point of View of Science and Faith.* London: James Nisbet, 1862. This contains one of the few able discussions of the relationship of the *testimonium* to the canon.

HAMILTON, NEILL Q. *The Holy Spirit and Eschatology in Paul.* Scottish Journal of Theology Occasional Papers No. 6. Edinburgh: Oliver and Boyd, 1957.

HARRIS, R. LAIRD. *Inspiration and Canonicity of the Bible.* Grand Rapids: Zondervan Publishing Co., 1957.

HEPPE, HEINRICH. *Reformed Dogmatics, Set Out and Illustrated from the Sources.* Foreword by Karl Barth; revised and edited by Ernst Bizer; English translation by G. T. Thomson. London: George Allen and Unwin, 1950. Excerpts from the Reformed dogmaticians.

131

HODGE, CASPAR WISTAR. "The Witness of the Holy Spirit to the Bible," *The Princeton Theological Review*, XI (1913), 41-84.

KLAIBER. "Die Lehre der altprotestantischen Dogmatiker von dem *testimonium spiritus sancti*, und ihrer dogmatischen Bedeutung," *Jahrbücher für Deutsche Theologie*, II/1 (1857) 1-54. This is one of the few specialized works on the *testimonium*. It is written from the Lutheran standpoint.

KRUSCHE, WERNER. *Das Wirken des Heiligen Geistes nach Calvin*. Göttingen: Vandenhoeck and Ruprecht, 1957. Excellent continental bibliography. This is a most thorough bit of Calvin research which is now indispensable for any work with Calvin or any work about the *testimonium*.

KUYPER, ABRAHAM. *Principles of Sacred Theology*. Grand Rapids: Wm. B. Eerdmans, 1954. This part of the famous Encyclopedia is one of the classic treatments of the *testimonium* and its place in theological methodology.

————. *The Work of the Holy Spirit*. New York: Funk and Wagnalls, 1900. This is a survey of systematic theology (virtually) from the perspective of the doctrine of the Holy Spirit. It is unsurpassed for its insights.

LECERF, AUGUSTE. *An Introduction to Reformed Dogmatics*. London: Lutterworth Press, 1949. This work by a great French Reformed theologian is a good parallel to the works of Kuyper and also shows the role of the *testimonium* in theological method.

————. "De l'autorité dans le calvinisme," *Études Calvinistes*. Paris: Delachaux et Niestlé, 1949, pp. 75-90.

LEO XIII, POPE. *On the Holy Spirit* [Encyclical, *Divinum illud*]. New York: The American Press, 1897.

LOETSCHER, W. "Luther and the Problem of Authority in Religion," *The Princeton Theological Review*, XI (1900), 55-65.

LUTHER, MARTIN. *A Commentary on St. Paul's Epistle to the Galatians*. Philip S. Watson, editor. London: James Clarke, 1953.

McGLOTHLIN, W. J. *Baptist Confessions of Faith*. Philadelphia: American Baptist Publication Society, 1911.

MASSELINK, WILLIAM. *General Revelation and Common Grace*. Grand Rapids: Wm. B. Eerdmans, 1953.

MURRAY, JOHN. "The Attestation of Scripture," *The Infallible Word*. Philadelphia: The Presbyterian Guardian Publishing Company, 1946, pp. 1-52. A straightforward presentation of the inspiration of Scripture and the inner witness of the Spirit.

NIESEL, WILHELM. *The Theology of John Calvin*. Translated by Harold Knight. Philadelphia: The Westminster Press, 1956. A short exposition of Calvin's theology by a continental Calvin expert and one of the editors of a new edition of Calvin.

OWEN, JOHN. *The Holy Spirit*. Grand Rapids: Kregel Publications, 1954.

PANNIER, JACQUES. *Le Témoignage du Saint-Esprit*. Paris: Librairie Fischbacher, 1893. One of the few specialized works on the *testimonium* but occasionally marred by intrusions of opinions of the French liberal school of Sabatier under whose direction this dissertation was written.

PATERSON, W. P. *The Rule of Faith.* New edition. London: Hodder and Stoughton, 1933. Considered to be one of the finest introductions to the comparative study of theology.

PRENTER, REGIN. *Spiritus Creator.* Philadelphia: Muhlenberg Press, 1953. This work is a detailed study of Luther's doctrine of the Holy Spirit and parallels Krusche's work on Calvin.

PREUS, ROBERT. *The Inspiration of Scripture. A Study of the Theology of the Seventeenth Century Lutheran Dogmaticians.* Edinburgh: Oliver and Boyd, 1955. This is a careful and sympathetic summary of the views of inspiration of the great Lutheran dogmaticians and shows how their views are frequently misrepresented.

RUPP, GORDON. "Word and Spirit in the First Years of the Reformation," *Archiv für Reformationsgeschichte,* XLIX (1958), 13-25. This is a very important article because it shows that the union of Word and Spirit preceded the *testimonium* historically.

SCHMID, HEINRICH. *The Doctrinal Theology of the Evangelical Lutheran Church.* Translated by Charles A. Hay and Henry E. Jacobs. 3d ed., revised. Philadelphia: Lutheran Publication Society, 1899. Contains excerpts from the great Lutheran dogmaticians and is a parallel to Heppe's work for the Reformed theologians.

STACKPOLE, EVERETT S. *The Evidence of Salvation or the Direct Witness of the Spirit.* New York: Thomas Y. Crowell, 1894. Although a very popular presentation, it is one of the very few works in English completely devoted to the *testimonium.*

STRATHMANN, *"martys, et. al.,"* in *Theologisches Wörterbuch zum Neuen Testament.* Stuttgart: Verlag von Kohlhammer, 1942. IV:477-520.

SWETE, HENRY BARCLAY. *The Holy Spirit in the Ancient Church.* London: Macmillan and Company, 1912. This is a basic study of the pneumatology of the Fathers.

WARFIELD, BENJAMIN. "Calvin's Doctrine of the Knowledge of God," *Calvin and Augustine.* Philadelphia: Presbyterian and Reformed Publishing Company, 1956, pp. 29-132. In many ways this is the finest presentation of the *testimonium* and an excellent view of Calvin's opinion. There is a trend in recent scholarship away from the classic Reformed view of Calvin and towards a more "neo-orthodox" interpretation of Calvin. This is a summons to renewed Calvin scholarship of the high order of Warfield.

WENLAND, H. "Das Wirken des Heiligen Geistes in den Gläubigen nach Paulus," *Theologisches Literaturzeitung,* LXXVII (1952), 457-470.

WHITAKER, WILLIAM A. *A Disputation on Holy Scripture.* The Parker Society. Cambridge: The University Press, 1844. This contains the Anglican defense of the *testimonium* against Romanism.

WITT, JOHN DE. "The Testimony of the Holy Spirit to the Bible," *The Presbyterian and Reformed Review,* VI (1895), 69-85.

SUBJECT INDEX

Apologetics, 13, 16, 128f.; and fundamentalism, 126
Apostles, as scribes, 32; as witnesses, 41
Athanasian Creed, 28
Authority, 65ff., 70f.

Baptists, 25
Believers, 87; possessors of word of God, 44; understand revelation, 54
Bibliolatry, 69

Canon, 93
Certainty, 16, 22, 49f., 65, 82, 85f., 106, 108
Christian consciousness, 50
Christian evidences, 117ff.; see also apologetics
Church, 79ff.; and subjectivism, 117; and word of God, 14
Conversion, 75
Crying, 51f., 67

Enthusiasts, 61
Eternal life, 60

Faith, 19, 49, 55, 70, 71, 95, 118
Fundamentalism, 65; and testimonium, 123ff.

God, as Father, 51ff., 74; as witness, 40, 41, 67
author of revelation, 53;
authority of, 70ff.;
granting illumination, 42;
incomprehensibility of, 16;
knowledge of, 35;
testimony of, 53, 59;
Gospel, 53, 88f., 101f.

Holy Scripture, 18, 31, 34, 44, and Holy Spirit, 57ff.;
and Roman Catholicism, 109ff.;
and testimonium, 42ff.;

as instrument of Holy Spirit, 58f., 63;
authority of, 65ff.;
autopistia of, 14, 20, 63;
dictation of, 32;
divinity of, 107f.;
inspiration of, 94;
majesty of, 14, 35;
no magical properties, 125f.;
sacramental view of, 25, 64, 125f.;
without Holy Spirit, 64;
written word of, 32, 33, 55f., 66, 67f., 73
Holy Spirit, and Christian consciousness, 29f.;
and cry of Father, 51f.;
and homoousian, 23;
and juridical terminology, 72;
and Pentecost, 77f.;
and the Trinity, 30f.;
and salvation, 47ff.;
and word of truth, 57ff.;
as internal minister, 17, 21;
as true witness, 59f.;
as wind of God, 91;
as witness, 41, 72ff., 91;
baptism of, 48;
dispensation of, 55f.;
image of in Scripture, 15;
persuasion of, 73;
signs of, 91;
tests for, 60f.
Human spirit, 51

Illumination, 23, 31ff., 42ff., 45, 46, 53, 63, 73, 75, 84ff., 93
Imago Dei, 37
Individualism, 80
Inner and outer word, 20
Intellectualism, 83

Jesuits, 25, 105
Jesus Christ, 17, 31, 33, 34, 42, 43, 44, 58

134

INDEX OF NAMES

INDEX OF SCRIPTURE